T0160431

CLOCKWISE FROM TOP: Mount Shasta
reflected in Heart Lake, a golden-mantled
squirrel, and Olberman's Causeway

CHRIS CARR/SHASTA MOUNTAIN GUIDES

CHRIS CARR/SHASTA MOUNTAIN GUIDES

CLOCKWISE FROM TOP LEFT: Crevasse rescue practice on Route 11: Hotlum Glacier, a climber stepping across a crevasse on Bolam Glacier, climbing a serac on Variation 11c: Hotlum Icefalls, climbers on the north side of Mount Shasta, skiing near Castle Lake, and climbing Variation 1b: Red Banks Chimneys

CHRIS CARR/SHASTA MOUNTAIN GUIDES

CHRIS CARR/SHASTA MOUNTAIN GUIDES

CHRIS CARR/SHASTA MOUNTAIN GUIDES

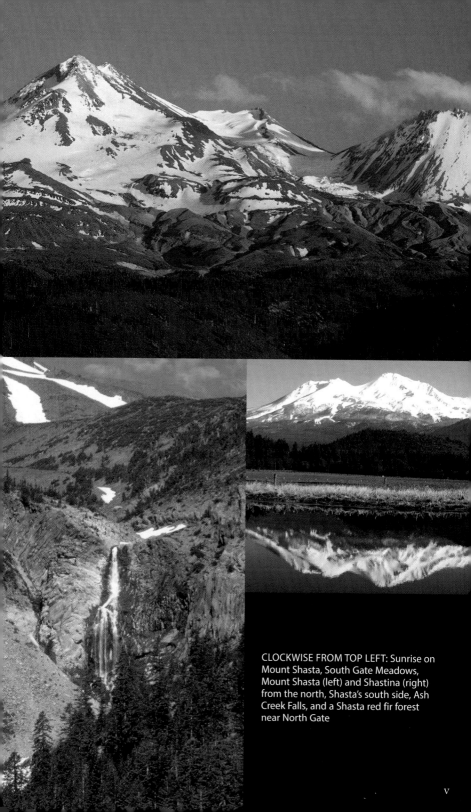

CLOCKWISE FROM TOP LEFT: Sunrise on Mount Shasta, South Gate Meadows, Mount Shasta (left) and Shastina (right) from the north, Shasta's south side, Ash Creek Falls, and a Shasta red fir forest near North Gate

CLOCKWISE FROM TOP LEFT: Descending Route 1: John Muir (Avalanche Gulch), climbing Route 5: Casaval Ridge, a Shasta lily, lenticular clouds above Mount Shasta, skiing down Route 10: Hotlum–Bolam Ridge, climbing Route 11: Hotlum Glacier, and sunset at the Bolam Glacier camping area

CHRIS CARR/SHASTA MOUNTAIN GUIDES

CLOCKWISE FROM LEFT: Route 5: Casaval Ridge, Clark's nutcracker, and approaching the summit of Mount Shasta circa 1985

CHRIS CARR/SHASTA MOUNTAIN GUIDES

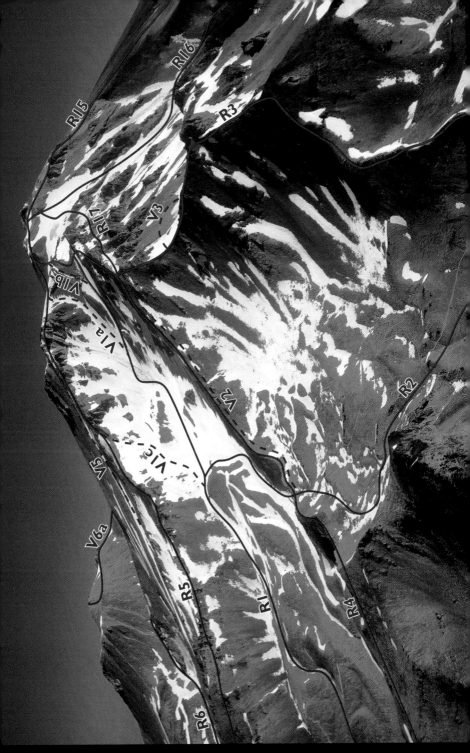

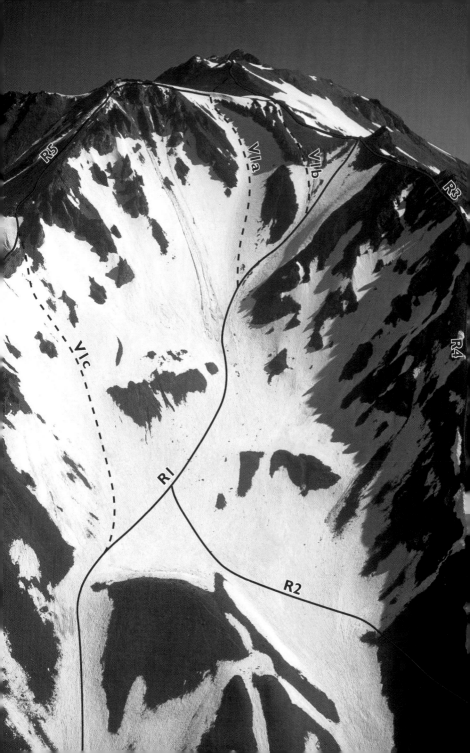

R6

V6b

V7a

V7b

R7

Whitney Glacier

Whitney Glacier (right), the Whitney–Bolam Ridge,
and the West Bolam Glacier (left)

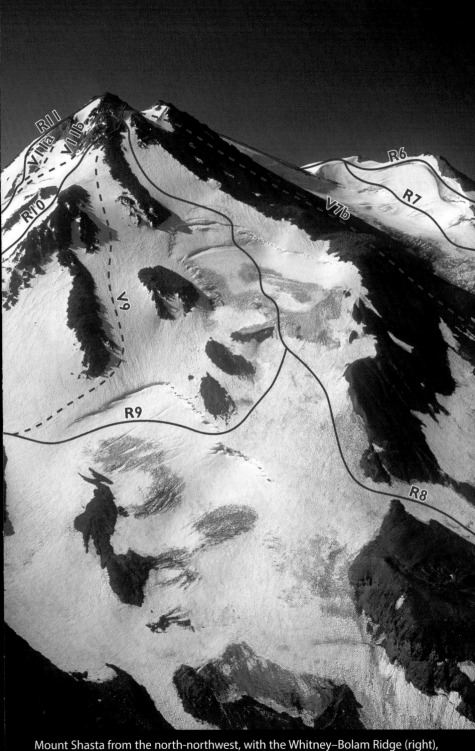

Mount Shasta from the north-northwest, with the Whitney–Bolam Ridge (right),
the Bolam Glacier, and the Hotlum–Bolam Ridge (left)

Mount Shasta from the north, with the Hotlum Glacier (center),
the Hotlum–Wintun Ridge, and Wintun Glacier (left)

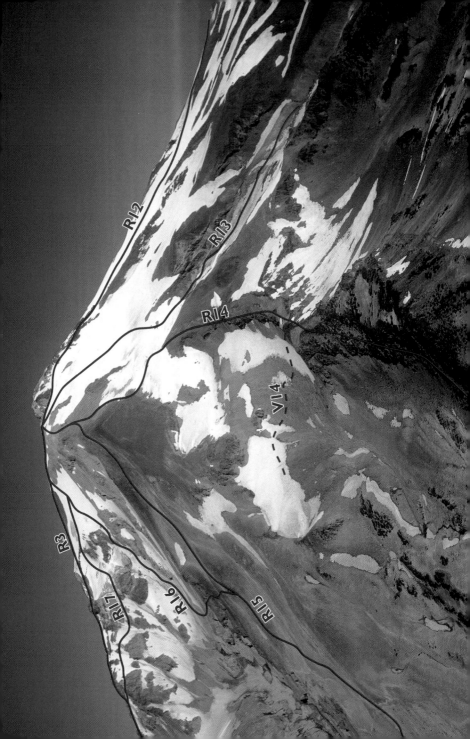

MOUNT SHASTA

A Guide to Climbing, Skiing, and Exploring
California's Premier Mountain

MOUNT SHASTA

A Guide to Climbing, Skiing, and Exploring
California's Premier Mountain

FOURTH EDITION

Andy Selters
Michael Zanger

 WILDERNESS PRESS ... *on the trail since 1967*

Mount Shasta
1st EDITION 1989
2nd EDITION 2001
3rd EDITION 2006
4th EDITION 2017

Cover and book design: Lora Westberg

Library of Congress Cataloging-in-Publication Data

Names: Selters, Andrew, author. | Zanger, Michael, 1941- author.
Title: Mount Shasta : a guide to climbing, skiing, and exploring California's premier mountain / Andy Selters, Michael Zanger.
Other titles: Mount Shasta book
Description: Fourth Edition. | Birmingham, Alabama : Wilderness Press, [2017] | "Distributed by Publishers Group West"—T.p. verso. | "3rd EDITION 2006"—T.p. verso. | Includes index.
Identifiers: LCCN 2017023346 | ISBN 9780899978666 (paperback) | ISBN 9780899978673 (ebook)
Subjects: LCSH: Hiking—California—Shasta, Mount (Mountain)—Guidebooks. | Mountaineering—California—Shasta, Mount (Mountain)—Guidebooks. | Skis and skiing—California—Shasta, Mount (Mountain)—Guidebooks. | Shasta, Mount (Calif. : Mountain)—Guidebooks.
Classification: LCC GV199.42.C22 S487 2017 | DDC 796.5109794/21—dc23
LC record available at https://lccn.loc.gov/2017023346

Manufactured in the United States of America

Published by: Wilderness Press
              An imprint of AdventureKEEN
              2204 First Ave. S, Ste. 102
              Birmingham, AL 35233
              800-443-7227; FAX 205-326-1012

Visit wildernesspress.com for a complete listing of our books and for ordering information. Contact us at our website, at facebook.com/wildernesspress1967, or at twitter.com/wilderness1967 with questions or comments. To find out more about who we are and what we're doing, visit blog .wildernesspress.com.

Distributed by Publishers Group West

Frontispiece: Heart Lake

SAFETY NOTICE: Though Wilderness Press and the authors have made every attempt to ensure that the information in this book is accurate at press time, they are not responsible for any loss, damage, injury, or inconvenience that may occur to anyone while using this book. You are responsible for your own safety and health while in the wilderness. The fact that a route is described in this book does not mean that it will be safe for you. Be aware that trail conditions can change from day to day. Always check local conditions and know your own limitations.

Contents

Trips by Type & Area xxii

List of Aerial Photos xxiv

Mt. Shasta Locator Map xxv

Acknowledgments xxvi

Introduction 1

A Primer to Climbing Mount Shasta 8

Weather 22

Climbing Routes 27

    Area: Southwest Side of Mount Shasta
    from Sargents Ridge to Cascade Gulch 30

    Area: Shastina to the Hotlum–Bolam Ridge 44

    Area: North and Northeast Sides: Hotlum and Wintun Glaciers 53

    Area: East and Southeast Sides: Clear Creek,
    Mud Creek Canyon, and Konwakiton Glacier 61

Skiing, Snowboarding, and Ski Touring 64

Hiking and Climber Access 82

Shasta's Geology 102

Shasta's Flora and Fauna 109

Amenities, Contacts, and Other Information 116

Afterword 122

Index 123

About the Authors 126

Trips by Type & Area

Climbing Routes

Area: Southwest Side of Mount Shasta from Sargents Ridge to Cascade Gulch

Route 1: John Muir (Avalanche Gulch) 30

Route 2: Old Ski Bowl 38

Route 3: Sargents Ridge. 39

Route 4: Green Butte Ridge 40

Route 5: Casaval Ridge. 41

Route 6: Cascade Gulch 42

Area: Shastina to the Hotlum–Bolam Ridge

Route 7: Whitney Glacier 44

Route 8: West Bolam Glacier 47

Route 9: East Bolam Glacier 48

Route 10: Hotlum–Bolam Ridge. 49

Area: North and Northeast Sides: Hotlum and Wintun Glaciers

Route 11: Hotlum Glacier 53

Route 12: Hotlum–Wintun Ridge. 56

Route 13: Wintun Glacier. 58

Route 14: Wintun Ridge. 60

Area: East and Southeast Sides: Clear Creek, Mud Creek Canyon, and Konwakiton Glacier

Route 15: Clear Creek 61

Route 16: Konwakiton Glacier from the East 62

Route 17: Konwakiton Glacier from the South 63

Skiing, Snowboarding, and Ski Touring

Route 1: John Muir (Avalanche Gulch) 69

Route 2: Old Ski Bowl 70

Route 4: Green Butte Ridge 70

Route 6: Cascade Gulch. 71

Route 7: Whitney Glacier. 71

Route 8: Bolam Glacier from the Northwest. 71

Route 9: Bolam Glacier from the Northeast 71

Route 10: Hotlum–Bolam Ridge.. 72

Route 11: Hotlum Glacier 72

Route 12: Hotlum–Wintun Ridge....................................... 72

Route 13: Wintun Glacier... 74

Route 14: Wintun Ridge... 74

Route 15: Clear Creek 74

Unplowed Everitt Highway, Bunny Flat to Old Ski Bowl 75

Old Ski Bowl.. 75

Tour to South Gate Meadows 75

Panther Meadow 75

Wagon Camp... 76

Gray Butte Northwest Face.. 76

Powder Bowl and Sun Bowl.. 76

Broadway 76

Bunny Flat Area.. 76

Horse Camp Area and Beyond 77

Horse Camp to McBride Springs 77

Sand Flat Area 77

Red Fir Flat 78

Ski-In Base Camps: Wilderness Skiing................................... 79

Lift-Serviced and Commercial Ski Areas 79

The Eddys, Castle Lake, and Beyond 80

Mount Shasta Ski Circumnavigation.................................... 80

Hikes on Shasta

Trip 1: Horse Camp Trail 88

Trip 2: South Gate Meadows Trail.. 93

Trip 3: Clear Creek Trail 93

Trip 4: Brewer Creek Trail 95

Trip 5: Ash Creek Falls Cross-Country Hike 95

Trip 6: North Gate.. 96

Trip 7: Whitney Falls... 98

Trip 8: Circum-Shasta Backpack 99

List of Aerial Photos

Shasta South. ix

Avalanche Gulch. x

Whitney xi

Bolam–Whitney. xii

Bolam xiii

Wintun–Hotlum xiv

Clear Creek–Wintun. xv

Mud Creek–Clear Creek xvi

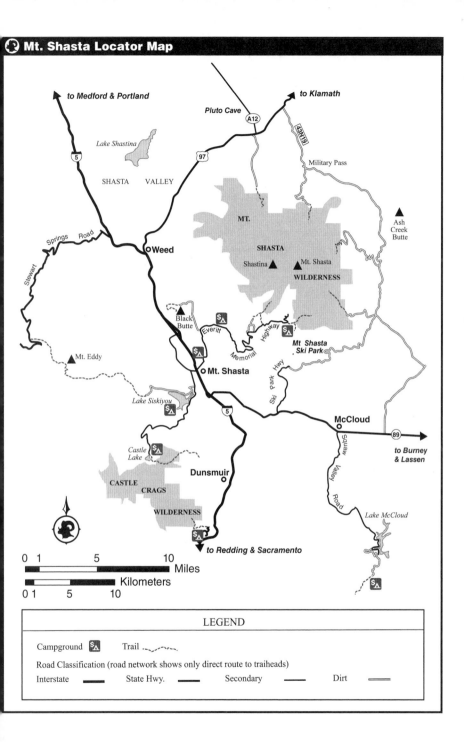

to Medford & Portland

to Klamath

Pluto Cave

A12

43N19

Lake Shastina

SHASTA VALLEY

5

97

Military Pass

Ash Creek Butte

MT. SHASTA WILDERNESS

Shastina

Mt. Shasta

Springs Road

Weed

Stewart

Black Butte

Everitt

Memorial

Highway

Mt Shasta Ski Park

Mt. Eddy

Mt. Shasta

Lake Siskiyou

Ski Park Hwy

McCloud

89

to Burney & Lassen

Castle Lake

Dunsmuir

CASTLE CRAGS WILDERNESS

Squaw Valley Road

Lake McCloud

0 1   5   10
Miles

0 1 5   10
Kilometers

to Redding & Sacramento

LEGEND

Campground   Trail

Road Classification (road network shows only direct route to traiheads)

Interstate   State Hwy.   Secondary   Dirt

Acknowledgments

Without the help and support of many of those who love Mount Shasta and associate themselves with the mountain, this book would have barely been possible. We would especially like to thank geologists Dan Miller, Paul Dawson, and Bruce Friend; botanist Dr. William Bridge Cooke; former College of the Siskiyous librarian Dennis Freeman; archaeologist and anthropologist Julie Cassidy; meteorologist Jim DePree; the Mt. Shasta Sisson Museum; Edward Stuhl; and the Bancroft Library.

Special thanks also go to Chris and Jenn Carr and Shasta Mountain Guides, wilderness rangers Nick Meyers and Forrest Coots, Tom Hesseldenz, Steve Johnson, Larry Jordan, Steven Labensart, Chris Marrone, Paul McHugh, Bill Miese, Jack Moore, Perry Sims, Chris and Sierra Zanger, and the folks at The Fifth Season . . . all mountain people at heart.

—Andy Selters and Michael Zanger

Bishop and Mt. Shasta, CA

2017

INTRODUCTION

For millennia Mount Shasta has spoken to people as a place of grandeur and inspiration in almost every imaginable way. This book is a collaboration between two mountaineers who have developed their own deep, personal relationships with Mount Shasta over the course of 80 combined years and counting. Like many others, we often measure our lives in terms of before and after we first encountered Mount Shasta.

For me (Michael), since the age of 5 I dreamed of and imagined beautiful snow-covered peaks. Many years ago I was on my way to Canada to climb and ski, and when I finally first saw Mount Shasta, it was like a dream come true. I hitchhiked up the Everitt Memorial Highway, and an elderly gentleman picked me up. It was the legendary Edward Stuhl—botanist, artist, mountaineer, and Shasta savant since the early 1900s. We immediately connected, and before we even reached the trailhead, he offered me the caretaker job at the Sierra Club Foundation's cabin at Horse Camp, the base camp for Shasta's popular John Muir (Avalanche Gulch) route. Meeting Ed Stuhl was the beginning of a life-changing mentorship. The Canada trip receded away, and before I even realized it, Mount Shasta became my home.

I've found that the mountains are a constantly renewing initiation and a window to the magic of the outdoors. In the mountains we test ourselves, find ourselves, and accept ourselves, and Mount Shasta is a

Skiing down Route 10: Hotlum–Bolam Ridge

superb and special setting for this journey. Even now, after scores and scores of climbs and endless explorations of the mountain, and all the perfect powder ski descents, and all the storms, and all the friendships, and all the nights on Shasta sleeping under the stars, I still ask myself: why am I not doing this more often?

For me (Andy), my Shasta awakening came just three weeks after escaping my youth of gasping with asthma in Los Angeles's smog. I had just started my freshman year at Humboldt State University, and I rode over with Phil Rhodes, another figure in the lineage of dedicated Shasta aficionados. He was leading our campus outing to climb both Shastina and Shasta. It was mid-January, and the best I could do for winter regalia was to slip cotton long johns under my jeans (not recommended). We arrived after dark, and I pressed against the window and saw a great, conical silhouette against the stars. "Wow," I said, "there it is." Phil glanced over and in his laconic way corrected me, "Oh, that's Black Butte. The real thing is a lot bigger."

I learned firsthand just how big and magnificent Shasta is. Seven of us followed Phil's lead to the top of Shastina, and then, on a skywalk, across the top of the Whitney Glacier toward the main summit. I couldn't believe how the gleaming slopes, so far above everything, resembled tales from Mount Everest. As we neared the top, though, something felt wrong, and along with two others I turned to go down a different route than what we had come up. Not until later did I realize I'd just gotten cold, too cold to think clearly about pulling my thick jacket out of my pack. I'd never been cold before and I'd gotten lucky; the mountain looked kindly on us. The inspiration and lessons from that trip steered me toward a lifetime of engaging mountains around the world, and many, many returns to Shasta. Each trip to Shasta is a blessing, and I will always think of it as my original teacher.

History of Discovery and American Indians

Mount Shasta stands in solitary dominance as the most striking mountain in Northern California. Its volume—estimated by various geologists to be between 84 and 120 cubic miles—makes it the most voluminous volcanic peak in the continental United States, larger than even Mount Rainier.

Its base-to-summit rise of more than 11,000 feet puts it in the company of very big mountains around the world. Mount Shasta's secondary cone, Shastina, would be the third-highest summit in the Cascade Range if it were separate from Shasta. Yet, Mount Shasta was the last major mountain of the Pacific Northwest to be discovered by European or American explorers. Rainier, Hood, St. Helens, and Baker were all named and mapped before 1800. Because Shasta was midway between the British settlements at Fort Vancouver (near the mouth of the Columbia River) and the Spanish enclaves in San Francisco and Monterey, explorers did not encounter it until they journeyed overland from these settlements nearly 300 miles into unknown territory.

It's possible, however, that earlier explorers may have come across the mountain while exploring the Pacific coastal region by sailing vessel. During the summer of 1786, French explorer Jean de La Pérouse, completing an exploration of the Pacific, sailed along the Northern California coast bound for the Spanish settlement at Monterey. His ship log for September 5 and 6 contained the following entry: "We then perceived a volcano on the summit of a mountain which bore east from us. The flame was very vivid; but a thick fog soon concealed it from our sight." Historians still disagree over what La Pérouse saw: a volcanic eruption or a large inland forest fire? Neither Mount Shasta nor Lassen Peak can be seen from the Pacific Ocean, but smoke and fire from a major eruption likely could have been visible. La Pérouse's maps and journals were sent to Paris before he set sail again from the San Francisco Bay area, but he was never able to explain the volcano he saw in greater detail, for the famous navigator, his ships, and its crews all disappeared in the South Pacific in 1788.

The early Spaniards in California occasionally sent out expeditions to search for mission sites or to assess the probability of foreign invasion. Two of the first inland explorations were led by Don Luis Antonio Argüello. In 1817 and 1821 he and his crew sailed up the Sacramento River in small boats, and missionaries on the trip noted the presence of a "very high hill called . . . Jesús María" and two mountains called Los Quates—"the Twins." According to historians, this reference suggests two possibilities. The first is that the party saw Mount Shasta and Lassen Peak. The second, more likely, explanation is that they saw Lassen Peak and its adjacent peak, Brokeoff Mountain. Argüello's journals hold few clues about how far north the company traveled, and historians still cannot say with any certainty that these early explorers saw Mount Shasta.

Next up was Peter Skene Ogden, a Hudson's Bay Company trapper who left Fort Vancouver on September 12, 1826. He journeyed east, and then down through central Oregon, eventually making his encampment at the rich trapping grounds of Klamath Marsh, east of Crater Lake, on December 12. Then, on February 14, 1827, while traveling northwest near the present California–Oregon border, Ogden made his now-famous journal entry: "I have named this river Sastise River. There is a mountain equal in height to Mount Hood or Vancouver, I have named Mt. Sastise. I have given these names from the tribes of Indians."

With this pronouncement, Ogden found favor with historians and was recognized as the discoverer and namer of Mount Shasta. However, later historians found some interesting discrepancies in the story. What the Early Hudson's Bay Company maps described as Mount Shasta and the Shasta River are known today as Mount McLoughlin and the Rogue River. Also, Shasta, an American Indian tribe that lived near the mountain, wasn't the tribe members' name for themselves, but the name the Klamath tribe used in referring to them. Later maps portrayed today's Mount Shasta variously as Mount Pitt, Mount Jackson, and Mount Simpson (the latter name reportedly given by frontiersman Jedediah Smith in honor of George Simpson, governor of the northwest Hudson's Bay territory). In 1846 Charles G. Nicolay wrote in his book *The Oregon Territory*: "Pitt Mountain, or, as it is called by the Americans, Mount Jackson, or as by the trappers Mount Shaste, is said to be 20,000 feet above the level of the sea."

In the early 1980s, archaeologist and historian Jeff LaLande retraced Ogden's route using his original journal records and concluded that Ogden had clearly followed Oregon's Rogue River and

PETER SKENE OGDEN

Peter Skene Ogden

had thus viewed Mount McLoughlin, which he named Mount Sastise. Though Ogden's maps have never been found, history has effectively granted him the title of first European-American discoverer of Mount Shasta. Whether he actually did remains a mystery to this day.

American Indians and Mount Shasta

Mount Shasta was the unmistakable physical and visual center for several American Indian tribes, and it was an integral part of the mythology of the native peoples who lived peaceful, insular lives within sight of the mountain. The largest tribes were the Shasta, Karuk, and Modoc to the north. The Wintun, Achomawi, and Atsugewi occupied lands to the southwest and east.

It was customary for great peaks to be regarded by American Indians as the starting point of their many boundaries, both geographical and spiritual. And, in spite of the differences among tribes in locations, language, and affiliations, each recognized Shasta as something of such immense grandeur that its existence could only be attributed to the Great Spirit, or Creator. The mountain, therefore, was also the tribes' spiritual center and thought to be the Great Spirit's wigwam. American Indian legends connected the material and spiritual worlds and described the powerful natural forces within the Shasta environment. The hot sulfur springs near Mount Shasta's summit are well known to climbers and a reminder that Shasta is a dormant volcano. It is not known if the

Mt. Shasta, 1863, by Juan B. Wandesforde *(courtesy of Turtle Bay Exploration Park)*

summit's hot springs were more prolific in earlier times, or if the mountain spewed enough steam and fumes to waft down into the valleys where the American Indians dwelled. Nevertheless, the Shasta tribe told a story of how the smoke and steam seen at the summit was the smoke hole of the Great Spirit's lodge, as well as the entrance to Earth.

Mount Shasta is still revered by American Indians. The upper springs at Panther Meadow, near the end of Everitt Memorial Highway on Shasta's southwest flank, are still used by Wintun medicine men and women for medicinal purposes and prayer. The Karuk tribe frequently conducts purification sweats at Sand Flat and other locations on the mountain. And elders from the tribes surrounding Mount Shasta still regularly recite traditional stories and songs.

Descending Hotlum Glacier

A PRIMER TO CLIMBING MOUNT SHASTA

If you hear a call to climb Shasta, you should know from your first look that this mountain is bigger than normal—by orders of magnitude. A Shasta climb is a strenuous journey up to a special island in the sky where the elemental ways of snow, ice, rock, and weather call the shots. It demands that we climb not just above the lowland plains but beyond our ordinary selves. While Shasta is a serious mountain, it is accessible to fit and savvy mortals, and hundreds of people succeed in climbing it every year. For many this is a beginning foray into alpine climbing, and for them especially, the mountain is a taskmaster that draws the line between a tremendous experience and a hard lesson. Accidents also happen every year, and, unfortunately, fatalities do too. To have a good climb and return whole and hearty, you need to work hard and long and pay attention. No book can substitute for mountaineering experience gained on earlier adventures, but in these pages we can help you start thinking like a mountaineer and envisioning the pyramid of skills you will need to rely on for a successful trip.

Physical Fitness and Training

To climb Shasta you need a strong foundation of endurance fitness. You will climb for one to three days, for a few to many hours each day—and when you're done going up, you'll need the juice to get back down. If you're starting from a sedentary lifestyle, you'll probably need to build up your endurance over several seasons of training.

The best training might be intrepid backpacking and climbs of lesser peaks in the Sierra and Cascades. For those tied to indoor schedules, a committed regimen of after-work running/cycling plus weekend mountain hiking can give you the basic fitness for a possibly successful ascent. Compared to urban workouts, though, a Shasta ascent requires a slower, steadier pace over a much longer time, so actual mountain outings offer much better training. On most of Shasta's routes the distance from a treeline camp to summit is barely more than 4 miles. The big effort, however, comes from rising about 7,000 feet into the thin air to reach an elevation of over 14,000 feet. Downhill training is necessary too; strong quads mean stable and healthy knees. Develop your preferences for your endurance-day diet as well.

Tenacity, Humility, and Judgment

Mountaineering is much more than an aerobic fitness challenge. On a big mountain like Shasta you need to manage hardships such as chilly morning wake-ups, long and sustained slopes, complex footing, variable weather, and more. The fitness of, say, a marathoner is without question a powerful aid, but even more valuable is the character to take on the tasks at hand with tenacity and humble honesty. Most of what mountaineers do is take care of the basics: staying warm, hydrated, fueled, and safely on the route. To that end, it's important to ration energy to stay alert to the terrain, the weather, and the team's condition, always saving some fuel for uncertainties and the descent. If you start a good-conditions summit day early, continue at a walking pace, and keep that one-step-at-a-time rhythm going, you'll be up to the top with plenty of time to savor the view and the triumph and get back down. If you try to gobble up the slopes with long strides and hurry, Shasta will grind your haste to a crawl.

Teammates and Team Awareness

Partnerships are as fundamental to mountaineering as fitness, and it behooves you to pay as much attention to your team as to your training. Good partnerships are as precious as gold, and they operate under an agreement that ensures 1) the group goes only as high as everyone in the party reasonably can, and 2) everyone comes back down safely. Ask yourself if you feel good about helping your teammates should they need assistance, and if they feel the same about you. If teammates stick together through thick and thin, the partnership will be better remembered than the summit. Few of us climb alone, and it's certainly ill-advised for beginners to consider that option. If you are new to mountaineering and you can't find trusted mentors or partners, contacting a guide service is a good idea.

Terrain Skills and Conditions Awareness

The best time to climb Shasta is when the slopes are covered with snow in good condition. What defines "good"? As Goldilocks might explain, just-right snow is firm but not icy and soft but not deep. Good snow conditions are most likely in the mornings and early afternoons of late spring and early summer—Shasta's preferred climbing season. Over the

Shastina (left) and Mount Shasta (right) from the south

course of several thousand feet and many hours of the sun's cycle you will encounter a range of conditions, though, and you need to be comfortable and in balance moving up, across, and down slopes in every possible condition. While it's not unusual to climb Shasta later in summer or fall when much of its snow has melted back to reveal a lot of rock (or even an entirely dry route), veterans recommend against climbing Shasta in dry conditions because it requires more work and there is more of a rockfall hazard.

You should be comfortable with the following alpine gear:

- sturdy, good-fitting mountain boots

- crampons that attach snugly and reliably to the boots

- a general, straight-shaft mountaineering ice ax of suitable utility and length—about 60–70 centimeters long for most people.

A helmet is also pretty much mandatory, as are gaiters—both to keep snow and scree out of your boots, and to hide laces and pants from the tripping catch of crampon points.

If you've never worn crampons before, you'll find the traction that they give on good snow is amazing, as long as you stay in balance. Pay attention to doing the basic climbing steps with balance and stability: keeping your head tall and over your feet, your feet turned to some degree across the slope, and the ankles flexing, in order to get as many crampon points as possible into the snow (not "edging"). With practice you can become amazingly secure on a slope of firm snow even when tired. To achieve optimal endurance and better balance, it's best to climb with shorter strides than you think, maintaining an upright posture and full-chest breathing along the way. If you feel good enough to go faster, don't start taking long strides; it's better to take those shorter strides with a quicker cadence.

You'll also want to practice holding and moving with your ice ax, your third point of a tripod. Taking your new gear out around your neighborhood may draw bewildered looks, but it's a good idea for beginners to start getting the feel for moving with boots, crampons, and an ax on a grassy or sandy slope. You'll also want to know how to deploy your ice ax to stop yourself should you fall (self-arrest technique). Classes and books teaching these basic alpine mountaineering skills can go a long way toward putting you on the right path.

As you climb you'll need to assess snow conditions. Successful Shasta climbers usually begin with a predawn start and a commitment to get back down by early afternoon. There are many advantages to this plan; perhaps the most important one is that it makes the best use of the daily snow cycle. In early morning, as you start up the lower-angle, lower-elevation slopes, ideally you'll find firm snow that the crampons bite into with security. By the time you reach steeper ground higher up, the sun should have softened the snow and made it more forgiving. When the snow gets much softer by midday or so, you'll already be into your descent. By midafternoon Shasta's snow can turn deeply mushy, and rockfall or loose-snow avalanches are more likely, so it's a good habit to be well down, off the mountain, or back in camp by then.

As the snow softens you may need to question whether to keep wearing the crampons or to continue with bare boots. When the snow gets deep—up to the ankles—or if the crampon points "ball up" with sticky snow, you're probably better off climbing with plain boots. Hot weather following a recent dump of new snow is usually what makes for sticky and deeper snow and strenuous postholing. Deep, wet snow can also be a sign of avalanche hazard and added reason to consider turning back. Conversely, if the snow is very firm or even icy, and steep enough that you don't feel secure or able to stop a possible fall, there is also ample reason to turn back. Sometimes an unusually cold day or a freezing rain can bring these difficult conditions even in prime climbing season; listen to your intuition to decide whether you're climbing on a navigable causeway or a dangerous sled run with consequences. On Shasta's north side in particular, during the latter half of summer, routes routinely harden with areas of glassy ice, making them too icy for average climbers to ascend safely.

Any long-lived climber learns to accept when conditions on a given day are not suitable. Delays happen to even the greatest; tough conditions are not your fault. You can't will a mountain to change, but you can retreat and come back when things are different. Climbing Shasta's slopes should make you feel like your hard work is being rewarded, with at most an occasional "uh, better watch out here" mixed in.

Weather Awareness

Mount Shasta is a pylon high in the atmosphere's flow, and up there you are incredibly exposed to the weather. On a fair, high-pressure day there might be few things more sublime than the view of hundreds of miles of Northern California and southern Oregon. When a real storm blows in with screaming winds, blizzard snow, or lightning, however, there are few things more desperate than a mountaineer trying to survive and escape to lower ground. In preparation, see the Weather chapter in this book, know what the weather outlook is before you start a climb, and plan accordingly.

Route Finding

As you climb you'll need to read the terrain and find your way from multiple perspectives. At the larger scale you should take in the overall route, and at the medium and smaller scales you'll have to choose passages that offer the best footing and travel. Studying the photos and map in this book will help with the larger and medium scales, as will checking out your route as soon as you can, including as you drive and hike

Lenticular clouds indicate strong winds up high.

to the base. For this, light binoculars are a fun and useful tool for picking out details, especially other climbers and their footsteps, icy areas, crevasses, and more. On the way up, periodically look back down to pay attention to what your descent will look like. On popular routes you may be relying on footsteps or nearby groups to help guide your way. Even if these provide accurate direction, it's important to know that you are responsible for your own route finding.

A GPS device can be helpful for finding the way across forgiving lower slopes to a trailhead or campsite, but high on the mountain it's imperative to know the entire route from start to finish, not just waypoints. The traditional route-finding devices of a good compass, altimeter, and map still work well up high. A compass can point the correct bearing to travel, and a calibrated, aneroid altimeter can help you keep track of key spots and tell you about how far you are from the top. Compasses need to be calibrated for the magnetic declination (14 degrees east at Mount Shasta), and altimeters must be calibrated to known, mapped elevations at least every few thousand feet.

Descending

Accidents happen more often on descent. When you're tired from the long climb, perhaps enthralled with success and ready to hurry back down, it can be easy to drop your guard. Add in deepening snow, changing weather, and your different perspective of the route as you head back, and problems can compound quickly. Route-finding errors, stumbles, and failing to see terrain traps like icy spots, cliffs, and crevasses can ruin a great trip.

Periodically rest and keep sipping and snacking to recover your alertness. Also breathe more. As we descend we are not stimulated to breathe as much as when we climb, so it's easy to get into a mildly hypoxic, dragging state. Remind yourself occasionally to take deep, deliberate breaths, and you'll move better.

Descending softened snow is much easier than descending rock. Heel-stepping and plunge-stepping can get you down Shasta's snowfields with efficient and happy ease. Keep your posture more forward and more over your feet than you might think, as leaning too far back can send your feet shooting out from under you. Recall any icy spots, crevasses, and rock areas you spotted on your climb up.

When you know the coast is clear with good snow, it can be useful to glissade—that is, to schuss down a snow slope. There are two basic ways to do this. The preferred, alpine way is to boot-ski. This works best when the snow is slightly soft, about midway through a daily melting cycle; skiing experience makes this more natural. Sun-cupped snow makes ski-booting more difficult, however, and by afternoon, as the snow softens more deeply, climbers sit down, spreading their body weight over a greater surface area. With their ax to one side as a ready brake, they ride on down. Stout, waterproof pants or pants with butt patches are helpful here. Beware, however, of slick shell clothing that can "grease" you out of control. In good conditions Shasta is rightly famous for magnificent sitting glissades that run for several thousand feet. Shasta is also infamous for glissading accidents. Stay in control; you wouldn't ride a bike down a hill without brakes, right? Only glissade when you know that your route below is clear with suitable snow, use your ax spike correctly to slow your speed, and be ready to flip over and deploy the ax to stop yourself. The many bad scenarios include hitting icy spots, sailing over cliffs or into crevasses, and crashing into rocks or partners. The most infamous mistake is to glissade with crampons still on; when the spikes catch, the leg gets injured. *Always take your crampons off.*

Trip-Planning Skills

Any mountain trip requires balancing what to bring with what to do without. Too much stuff in your pack makes you work too hard and can slow you down to the point of being dangerous, while forgetting something important can bring your trip to a standstill. Seasoned backpackers used to covering lots of miles and elevation changes in different seasons should have a good idea of what clothing, food, and camping gear to carry on Shasta.

The adjustments to make for high-altitude climbing include more water (2–4 quarts on a long day), more sunscreen, and clothing layers (including gloves) for a wide range of temperatures. On Shasta you always want good shell clothing and a reserve layer that insulates even when wet.

To Camp or Not to Camp

For most climbers Shasta is too big of a bite for a day trip. The most common itinerary starts with a hike in to a camp near treeline, at about 8,000 feet. Getting there usually takes an hour to maybe 3 or 4. Reaching an even higher camp, at say 9,000 or 10,000 feet, usually takes a few to several hours. Take-it-easy climbers can plan on taking two days to reach the higher camp. Taking smaller bites of a climb over more days makes for a more relaxed experience in theory, except that carrying a heavier pack up to that higher camp is hard work, and at higher elevations many people don't sleep as well. Whatever itinerary you choose, planning for it and anticipating what it takes will bring you the best chance for success.

High Altitude

It's also important to plan for Shasta's altitude. The air on Mount Shasta's summit, 14,179 feet way up in the sky, is 40% thinner than it is at sea level. This means that the sun burns down that much more fiercely, and—most significantly—there's 40% less oxygen. Even at 10,000 feet there's 30% less oxygen. Rapid exposure to this reduced oxygen level can make any of us sick, and if the sickness isn't treated by going down to find richer air, we can get very sick indeed.

The sky above Mount Shasta

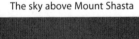

Doctors refer to basic altitude illness as acute mountain sickness, or AMS. The symptoms are some combination of lassitude, headache, and nausea, along with a racing pulse and strained breathing. AMS is different than fatigue, and your level of fitness is no safeguard against it. This is an important point: fitness can help you climb better, *but fit people get AMS just as easily as anyone else.*

There are two basic strategies to work with the altitude challenge. One is to make a gradual ascent over several days, allowing our bodies to adjust. The other is to make a relatively quick ascent and descent— over just one or two days—with the idea that climbers will get up and back down before altitude sickness comes on. In practice, most Shasta climbers, knowingly or not, count on a modest degree of acclimatization and returning to lower altitudes before getting sick. Many or even most Shasta climbers start feeling at least a little crummy and slower at some point above 12,000–13,000 feet. The question can then become: is everyone in the party doing well enough to keep going up and get back down in a reasonable time, or will continuing up compound your slowing pace to a point of real trouble?

For your body to start acclimatizing, it's helpful to spend a first day and night at around 7,000–8,000 feet. This is high enough to start challenging your system and stimulating acclimatization but not high enough to make you sick. Within a couple of hours after arriving there, you'll likely feel a bit shorter of breath. Take an easy hike, and sleep under the stars. Those who then camp a second night at this location, or a little higher, at 9,000–10,000 feet, will likely be better acclimatized and feel better on their summit day.

For a susceptible minority, though, sleeping at 10,000 feet or so on the second night can bring on AMS. This is because it's often the sleeping altitude that brings on the illness. While getting used to altitude, *never* take sleeping pills to help with sleeping or manage a headache—these medicines depress breathing and are an easy ticket to life-threatening high-altitude illness.

There are a few other things you can do to help. One, don't try to go faster than your steady breathing allows. Oxygen-sucking sprints often bring on an AMS cycle. Two, drink plenty of water, more than you would with sea-level exertion, and enough to keep your pee copious and almost clear. Your lungs lose lots of water as you breathe hard in thin air,

A team returning from the summit at Horse Camp in a July snowstorm

and dehydrated tissues are more susceptible to AMS. Three, monitor for AMS symptoms, and check in with your body especially at a rest stop. If a decent sit-down and drink makes you feel refreshed, great. If you don't feel rested or in fact you feel worse—and especially if you have a headache and the thought of eating or drinking is repulsive—there's a good chance you're suffering from AMS. The only steps for treatment are steps downhill, back down to richer air. Monitor your partners too.

Use of a Rope

Nothing ties a team together like a rope. However, to paraphrase a famous Scottish climber, there's nothing like a rope to ensure that in a fall everyone tumbles together. Shasta's more difficult routes have snow-covered crevasses and steep and sometimes icy slopes that call for competent roped travel or belayed climbing. For typical Shasta climbers in most conditions, routes in this book rated D1 are not difficult enough to require roped climbing. Routes rated D2 may require roped climbing, and D3 routes are steep and technical enough that most climbers will want to deploy a rope. If you don't know what competent roped climbing means, stick to the least-difficult routes.

Rockfall

Like all the volcanoes in the Cascade Range, Shasta is made up of volcanic rock mixed with cinders and ash. Various acidic volcanic compounds can at times weaken this messy combination, resulting in a lot of loose and crumbling stone. Add in the melting and freezing of snow and occasional high winds, and you have a mountain that likes to shed its rocks. Rocks can and do tumble down unpredictably on occasion, but most of the time there are patterns to their falls and specific places where climbers can find relative safety. Alpine wisdom is to get up and down a mountain before the hot afternoon sun starts melting snow enough to carry rocks off, and to climb earlier in the season, when most rocks are buried under snow. This general advice applies on Shasta.

Rescue

Climb with a warrior's assumption of self-sufficiency: go up expecting that you and your party are on your own, even should things go awry. Should something indeed go wrong, basic first aid skills and cool-headed team-work can bring lightly injured or ill-feeling people back down to safety. Self-sufficiency has long been a fundamental aspect to mountaineering, especially in North America. Think twice before asking others to drop what they are doing and potentially endanger themselves to help you.

When something goes wrong that a team can't handle, responders are available. The way to get help is to call 911. Cell phone service does not reach the entire mountain, though, and it's particularly spotty on the north side. Because of this, and many other variables, the plain truth is that rescuers may or may not be able to come swiftly.

WEATHER

Mount Shasta is known worldwide for its towering lenticular clouds—those lens-shaped giants that park over the summit like a stack of galactic pancakes. Shasta's winds are also legendary, and during prolonged winter storms aircraft give the mountain a wide berth while climbers and skiers stay indoors. In the summer, billowing cumulus thunderheads can form quickly during the afternoon, sometimes producing thunderstorms before sundown.

Nearly all of us who have hiked, camped, or climbed have heard the expression "Mountains make their own weather." In a sense, this is true. But in reality, mountains—and Mount Shasta is a prime example—are simply displaying weather changes earlier than the surrounding lowlands.

Certain weather signs on Mount Shasta give us clues to approaching weather changes and storms. Storms usually move into the Shasta area with a southwest flow, and the first indication of an approaching storm is a change in wind direction from the prevailing north or east to winds from the southwest. Wind speed is also likely to increase. Another sign of an approaching storm is the moisture content of the air, as indicated by cloud formations. The leading edge of a storm usually presents high clouds—cirrus and cirrostratus. These clouds thicken and lower as the storm nears. Low-level moisture is indicated by Mount Shasta's famous lenticulars and other less-defined cap clouds. Before storm clouds completely blanket the sky, the top of Mount Shasta will usually be swathed in a thick cap cloud, which will descend as the storm approaches. Temperatures may be relatively warm before the cap cloud forms but will fall dramatically once it is in place.

Many hours—or only a few—may elapse from the time a storm's leading edge reaches Shasta until low clouds collect and precipitation begins. If towering cumulus clouds are visible as the storm approaches, the window will usually be short, and thunderstorms may occur along with gusty winds, lightning, hail, and other severe weather.

If you're climbing or hiking on Mount Shasta below a cap cloud, observing the cloud's actions can be very helpful in forecasting weather changes. For example, if the cap stays above 12,000 feet, the storm may not get worse. Winds will remain high, but the cap cloud may even begin to diminish. If the cap cloud thickens and descends, the storm will probably worsen, and descent from the mountain is advisable. When a storm forms quickly, such as an afternoon thunderstorm, its duration is usually brief—sometimes only a few hours. But if a storm takes one or more days to develop, it can often last for several days before dissipating.

The latest weather information for the Shasta area is available from the following sources:

- The Fifth Season outdoor shop 24-hour climbing report: 530-926-5555

Mount Shasta Weather Websites:

- wunderground.com (enter "Mount Shasta, CA")

- weather.com (enter "Mount Shasta, CA")

- mountain-forecast.com (enter "Mount Shasta")

- shastaavalanche.org (many useful links)

- avalanche.org (click on "Mt. Shasta")

Cumulus clouds stretching high above Mount Shasta can be innocuous, but they can also build into dangerous thunderstorms.

Route 11: Hotlum Glacier

CLIMBING ROUTES

Though a great mountain like Shasta has special rewards for those who venture onto it, life on the heights is not always easy, and our goals may be hard to achieve. Certainly, even the best mountaineers and other outdoorsmen have known discomfort, difficulty, and even fear. In fact, knowledge and understanding of adversity are what set seasoned adventurers apart from those with less experience.

The enjoyment, challenge, and satisfaction of climbing should always be tempered with concern for safety. This book can help you discover some wonderful, exciting places on Mount Shasta, but it's no substitute for experience, careful preparations, and good judgment. You are responsible for your own safety. To ensure it, you must get proper mountaineering training and then exercise caution and common sense based on that training plus experience. Many outdoor organizations and clubs, as well as college and university recreation programs, offer mountaineering courses. These courses are a good way to learn climbing from experienced climbers.

Shasta displays many changes and many moods over the seasons. A climb along the John Muir (Avalanche Gulch) route during the long, calm days of early summer is usually sublime. The same climb in winter can be very serious and difficult. During ample snow years, many of the north-side and eastside routes remain in excellent condition with hard snow throughout the summer and fall. However, in drier years, and generally by autumn of normal years, they can become glassy ice. We recommend that you always check weather and snow conditions before starting a hike or a climb. We also urge you to be honest with yourself and your climbing partners regarding your goals, experience, gear requirements, and even your mind-set. Mountains must be met on their own terms. Therefore, take responsibility for your judgment, actions, and welfare.

Many emergencies and fatalities have occurred on Mount Shasta, and rescue is often lengthy, dangerous, and uncertain. Rescues may be delayed by unfavorable weather, unavailability of helicopters able to fly in the thin air of the upper altitudes, hazards to rescuers, and other problems.

The Siskiyou County Sheriff's Department is responsible for coordinating rescue efforts on Mount Shasta, but unless it knows an accident has occurred, it will not take action until *after* your expected return date has passed. Your wilderness permit information can be utilized for rescue purposes, but it is not a rescuer's document and there is no sign-out.

We've chosen what we think are the finest routes on Mount Shasta, along with some selected variations. The route descriptions are fairly general—partly because the mountain is never quite the same from season to season and partly so as not to deprive you of the sense of adventure. Many of the routes do not require a rope, but most require an ice ax and crampons, as well as knowledge of their use. Other routes require more experience, specialized equipment, glacier training, and crevasse rescue knowledge. Some of the summit routes are quite long if started from base camp, so we've mentioned some high camps to break the climb into shorter days if you choose. The climbing routes are listed clockwise around the mountain, beginning on the southwest side at the historic John Muir (Avalanche Gulch) climb.

Note that *season* typically refers to snow levels and conditions, not necessarily the time of year.

Climbing Difficulty Ratings

Difficulty ratings for climbing routes are a very subjective topic. They reflect typical climbing conditions, which are always subject to change. During storms or icy conditions, for instance, a climb can be more difficult than the rating implies.

There is no universally accepted rating system in North America for climbs on alpine peaks such as Mount Shasta. Thus, we (the authors) developed an ad hoc D1–D3 rating system (see below) to apply only on Mount Shasta, showing the relative difficulty of the peak's routes.

D1, 3rd class: Moderate terrain and moderate conditions, either rock or snow, requiring proper footwear, an ice ax, and crampons. A rope is generally not needed but may be taken for less experienced members or icy conditions.

> *Examples: Route 1 John Muir (Avalanche Gulch)*
> *Route 15 Clear Creek*

D2, 4th class: A rope is necessary for belaying and protection, but the climbing is not overly difficult. Traveling on crevassed glaciers may be necessary, but the terrain and route finding are moderate.

> *Examples: Route 5 Casaval Ridge*
> *Route 8 West Bolam Glacier*

D3, 5th class: Difficult ice and snow or rock requiring specialized equipment and advanced technique. The glaciers may have steep ice-falls, many crevasses, and difficult route finding.

> *Example: Route 11 Hotlum Glacier*

Shastina (left) and Mount Shasta (right)

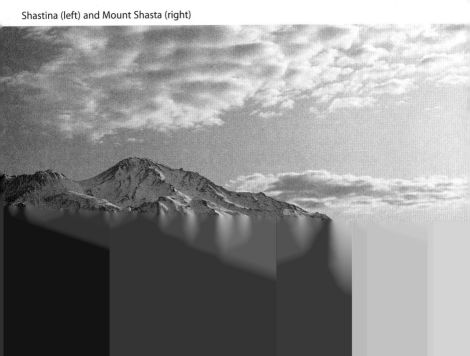

First Ascent

On August 14, 1854, Elias D. Pearce of nearby Yreka led a group of seven friends up Shasta's southwest flank, accomplishing the first ascent. They marked the occasion by planting a large American flag at the summit. The doubting public, who still thought Mount Shasta was impossible to climb, did not believe Pearce's success. Pearce therefore organized a second climb to prove his claims, and on September 19, 1854, eight climbers, led again by Pearce, stood on Shasta's summit. Pearce succinctly remarked after his second successful climb: "There was no longer any doubt of the accessibility of the summit of Shasta Butte; though should one stand at its base and view its rugged form and towering peak, they would readily pronounce its ascent impossible."

The veil of impossibility had been lifted from Mount Shasta, and other ascents quickly followed Pearce's two climbs. From 1854 to 1856 no fewer than 40 people (5 women and 35 men) ascended the mountain. The first woman to climb Mount Shasta was Harriette Catherine Eddy, for whom nearby Mount Eddy is named.

Southwest Side of Mount Shasta from Sargents Ridge to Cascade Gulch

ROUTE 1 John Muir (Avalanche Gulch) ➤ See map, p. x
DIFFICULTY: D1
ACCESS: Everitt Memorial Highway via Bunny Flat (N41° 21.233' W122° 13.967') or Sand Flat (N41° 20.783' W122° 14.617')
CAMPSITES: Horse Camp, Helen Lake, Sand Flat, Bunny Flat
TIME: 1 day

Elias D. Pearce used this route in 1854 for the first recorded ascent of Mount Shasta, and it quickly became the route for the overwhelming majority of ascents. A few decades later, it became common to refer to it as the John Muir route, honoring the famous naturalist who began a love affair with Shasta in 1874 (see the sidebar on page 35). During the 20th century, though, this route became known by the geographic feature Avalanche Gulch, which has led to misperceptions that the route is prone to avalanches. During winter and spring this route can indeed avalanche, but no more often than other aspects of the mountain. Muir's legacy is the best one to memorialize this, still the most popular route on Shasta.

In the early days, a climb began on horseback in Strawberry Valley in the town of Sisson, which was later named Mt. Shasta. Guides and outfitters would then lead their parties to a timberline base camp near the site of the present-day Sierra Club Foundation cabin at Horse Camp. Here, horses could graze and drink in pastoral peace while a party climbed.

Over the years, increased use of this area brought improvement of the trail, establishment of campsites, and, in 1922, construction of the Sierra Club Foundation's stone cabin. From then through 1934, the cabin's first custodian, Mac Olberman, built a "causeway" of huge flagstones to start climbers on the route. With just these enhancements, Horse Camp remains a historical and pleasant place today. Climbers the world over still gather with a sense of camaraderie, a summer custodian still stays at the cabin to help first-time visitors, and the evening views out to the Trinity Alps are still the catalysts of tall tales. From the stone benches lining the rear wall of the cabin, you can scout many features of this climbing route. This is a wonderful base camp for one's first climb on Mount Shasta.

It is only 4.1 miles from the Sierra Club Foundation cabin to the summit but more than 6,000 vertical feet! From a viewpoint just behind the cabin, the foreground vista (and the beginning of the climb) can be divided into three areas, from left to right: the climber's gully, the middle moraines, and Avalanche Gulch. Olberman's Causeway, laboriously built of huge, flat stones by the cabin's first custodian, Mac Olberman, begins just a few feet behind the cabin and leads you in the proper direction.

Follow the causeway as it heads toward the peak. (When the causeway is still covered with snow, ascend the broad, main drainage behind the cabin.) Continue up the long climber's gully, which curves left, straightens, and then opens up to a broad area of gentle flats and rock moraine. You are now to the left (west) of the huge, open drainage called Avalanche Gulch. Ascend moderate slopes to a flat area at 10,400 feet known as Helen Lake. You can also reach Helen Lake by ascending the morainal hills, just right (east) of the climber's gully. This line is a little more direct but also steeper in places. Conditions at the time will dictate the best choice; consolidated snow is always easier climbing than loose talus. Few climbers use Avalanche Gulch proper as a means of ascent to Helen Lake, but it's often an excellent ski descent route.

Helen Lake was named in 1924 when Helen Wheeler, guided on a successful summit climb by Ed Stuhl, inquired about the name of the lovely tarn. Ed christened the tiny lake on the spot, and the name has stuck ever since. Actually, the lake is usually under snow and hence seldom seen except late in exceptionally dry years. During periods of drought, snows melt back enough to reveal Helen Lake as a genuine body of water.

If you wish to establish a higher base camp than Horse Camp, the bench at Helen Lake is a popular but often crowded site. Except in winter and early spring, runoff water is usually available, and a number of flat, protected campsites have evolved over the years. Increased use of this fragile alpine environment necessitated a human waste pack-out policy by the U.S. Forest Service. Better protected, less windy, and less crowded campsites exist at the 9,600- to 9,800-foot level, below Helen Lake.

Above Helen Lake lies the most strenuous section of the route, a 2,500-foot snowfield that steepens to 35 degrees near its top. Stay right of center of the main drainage, aiming generally toward the right side of the Red Banks, the prominent orange palisades of welded pumice that represent one of Shasta's more recent volcanic flows. Constant vigilance is advised as the Red Banks are the source of most of the rockfall in Avalanche Gulch. Allow yourself plenty of time to climb and return before the sun's heat can loosen and dislodge any rocks. Mid- to late summer is the most dangerous time, though rockfall can occur during any season and at any time. At nearly 12,000 feet, continue climbing to the right of a large rock field called the Heart. Depending on the time of the year and the previous winter's snowpack, this rock feature can take on a variety of sizes and shapes. The Heart can also be a source of rockfall. Generally, climbing farther south (climber's right) in this drainage results in the least exposure to rockfall. The small saddle between the Red Banks and Thumb Rock at 12,800 feet is a good place to rest, eat, and warm up in the sun; a snug alcove can provide protection in case of wind.

There are two main options for the next section: either around or through the Red Banks. The usual way is to walk briefly around and behind the Red Banks on the edge of the Konwakiton Glacier, avoiding the crevasse (often called a bergschrund, though technically it's a moat here) where the glacier snow has pulled away from the rock. In mid- to late summer the bergschrund can be quite large, blocking easy return to the Red Banks' crest. Snowbridges across this bergschrund may offer safe passage in the cool of morning, but be aware that they can be dangerously softened by the afternoon sun.

If a lack of equipment and experience or plain intuition causes doubt about going around the Red Banks, you can backtrack a few hundred feet and climb through one of several gullies in the Red Banks, reaching their top shortly. Depending on seasonal conditions, short but steep snow slopes, ice, and exposure on this section through or around the Red Banks can be the one area on this route where some climbers might want the comfort of a rope, but unless a partner is skilled in anchoring and holding falls in the conditions present, a rope can add a false sense of security and the potential to pull off teammates.

Whichever route you choose to ascend the Red Banks, continue climbing along the top of the Red Banks and follow the ridge to its top, a broad snowfield bounded on the north by the Whitney Glacier and on the south by the Konwakiton Glacier.

Coauthor and ice-climbing pioneer Andy Selters on steep water ice in a Red Banks gully in wilder days, late 1970s. Climbing ice without a roped belay or helmet is not recommended.

A worthwhile side trip is a brief walk north on the snowfield at the top of the Red Banks. Here, you can enjoy a view of the whole expanse of the Whitney Glacier, the longest glacier in California. In midseason, Clarence King Lake (within Shastina's crater) and Sisson Lake (on the saddle between Shasta and Shastina) appear as turquoise jewels against the stark white backdrop of snow.

Beyond the Red Banks continue up Misery Hill (either a misnomer or an understatement, depending on conditions of the route and condition of the climbers) via the best-quality snow or a faint scree trail to the slope's right of center. You soon reach the flat summit snowfield. Cross this plateau, heading for an obvious col (saddle) between the summit pinnacle to the right (east) and a smaller one to the west. Wind and sun often sculpt the summit snowfield into a labyrinth of bizarre and beautiful shapes called *penitentes*. During late season, and in years of light snowpack, the twisted cylindrical remains of the old geodetic monument may be seen emerging from snow beneath the southwest face of the summit pinnacle. The bubbling sulfur fumaroles nearby are a reminder that Mount Shasta is indeed a volcano, active not long ago.

Ascend the summit via easy scrambling on its northwest side, thus concluding Mount Shasta's most historic and most popular route. Descend via the same route.

Variation 1a Left of Heart ➤ See map, p. x
DIFFICULTY: D2
TIME: 1+ days

During unusually dry seasons, and late in the summer, this drainage typically holds snow longer than the traditional route to the right, offering better climbing for those who are experienced on steep slopes. Climb increasingly steep snowfields above Helen Lake until you're beneath the imposing north end of the Red Banks.

Depending on seasonal conditions, several icy chimneys offer challenging passages through these palisades, and in fact ice climbers looking for rare summer practice can often find some near-vertical water ice in some of them. The chimneys become shorter and easier the farther left (north) you go along the Red Banks, though steep snow cornices often overhang at the extreme left end. If so, a steep, short ridge left (north) of the Red Banks abuts the very top of Casaval Ridge and offers passage

John Muir

George Grantham Bain Collection (Library of Congress)

John Muir

John Muir, perhaps the most eloquent and peripatetic naturalist the world has known, first saw Mount Shasta from the Sacramento River canyon during the early fall of 1874. Of that moment, he later wrote: "When I first caught sight of it . . . I was fifty miles away and afoot, alone and weary. Yet all my blood turned to wine, and I have not been weary since."

In the following weeks Muir climbed Mount Shasta, walked around the base of the mountain, and visited Black Butte and Shasta's glaciers— all the while making notes for future articles, letters, and essays.

The next year Muir was asked to take barometric and temperature readings on Shasta's summit for the U.S. Coast and Geodetic Survey and its proposed summit monument. Muir, with friend and guide Jerome Fay, climbed the mountain on April 30, 1875. As Muir recounts in one of his most famous essays, the tasks of measuring, as well as Muir's fascination with building clouds, caused them to linger on the summit. Based on his Sierra experience, Muir did not expect what happened next. "The storm at once became inconceivably violent," as hail and snow pelted them, winds roared, and the temperature dropped below zero. Declaring that they could not escape down the mountain, Fay had them take "shelter" by lying in the mud of the summit's sulfurous hot springs. There they stayed, alternately scalding on one side and freezing on the other as they turned over and over into the night. The stars came out, and in the morning Muir and Fay made their way down, scarcely able to bend their frozen trousers.

Muir worked tirelessly for the establishment of national parks and recreation areas. Mount Shasta remained a favorite haunt, and he called it "the polestar of the landscape."

Ed Stuhl: A Lifetime with Mount Shasta

Ed Stuhl

In June 1917 Edward Stuhl walked up the same Sacramento River canyon that John Muir had traveled 40 years earlier. When he reached the area in the canyon near Dunsmuir where Muir had first sighted Mount Shasta, Stuhl was equally overcome. Thus began a lifelong association with Mount Shasta. Stuhl grew up in Austria and spent his summers traveling through the Austrian mountains for his father's stained glass studio, repairing church windows that had suffered winter storm damage. Years later he recalled that a turning point in his life occurred when he saw the original "Buffalo Bill" Cody and Annie Oakley's "Wild West Show" in Munich, kindling a desire to experience the American West.

around the cornices. You are now atop the Red Banks and at the base of Misery Hill, slightly north of the traditional route, which can be followed to the summit.

Descend the same route or Route 1.

Variation 1b Red Banks Chimneys See map, p. x
DIFFICULTY: D2
TIME: 1 day

When the Konwakiton Glacier bergschrund presents difficulties (see Route 1 description), these variations are enjoyable, time-saving detours.

Ed and his wife, Rosie, made their way to California, and from 1929 to 1946 they worked for William Randolph Hearst at the publisher's famous Wyntoon estate along the McCloud River. During this time Stuhl successfully climbed Mount Shasta many times, assisted with the construction of the Sierra Club Foundation cabin at Horse Camp, and indulged his passion of creating beautiful watercolor paintings of Mount Shasta's wildflowers. For years he was the de facto custodian of the cabin, and his campfire stories enthralled the many climbers and hikers who met him on the mountain.

The Stuhls later settled in a log cabin west of the town of Mt. Shasta and lived actively until well into their 90s. They both skied until their 80s, and Ed—who climbed every major mountain in Washington, Oregon, California, and Mexico—made a solo winter climb of Mexico's 17,797-foot Popocatépetl when he was 73.

Ed's great hope was to see Mount Shasta preserved as a national or state park or as a wilderness area. He died in 1984 at age 97, only a few months before the U.S. Congress designated the Mt. Shasta Wilderness. Two legacies of Ed live on: a wildflower guidebook of his exquisite Mount Shasta wildflower paintings and the love and appreciation of Mount Shasta that he instilled in everyone he met.

When climbing the traditional route (Route 1), you pass beneath the Red Banks for several hundred feet before reaching a saddle at Thumb Rock. At the lowest point of the Red Banks is a huge, cleft rock outcrop that looks like a caricature valentine. Just right of this "heart" (not the same as the rock island below of that name) is a deep, snow-filled chimney leading all the way to the top of the Red Banks. A few hundred feet right of this chimney is another landmark—an anvil-shaped rock. This rock may also be passed on either side to reach the top of the Red Banks.

Descend via Route 1—though the chimneys may be descended if they are not too icy.

Variation 1c Upper Casaval Ridge ➤ See map, p. x
DIFFICULTY: D2–D3
TIME: 1+ days

Looking north from Helen Lake, you can see a broad shoulder descending from Casaval Ridge. This shoulder is much less steep than any other rib or gully descending from Casaval Ridge. It is the second window, a common escape, or bailout, from Route 5. This route variation also makes an excellent portal for gaining access to the upper reaches of Casaval Ridge late in the season when the lower parts of the ridge lack snow. Follow Casaval Ridge to its top, then take the traditional route (Route 1) to the summit.

Descend either your ascent route or Route 1, depending on conditions and time.

ROUTE 2 Old Ski Bowl ➤ See map, p. ix
DIFFICULTY: D1
ACCESS: Everitt Memorial Highway via Panther Meadow (N41° 21.717' W122° 12.033')
CAMPSITES: Panther Meadow, Old Ski Bowl lodge parking area
TIME: 1 day

The original Mt. Shasta Ski Bowl opened in 1959, and it remained in operation until 1978, when weather, financial problems, and a lift-destroying avalanche forced its closure. All that remains is the parking lot. While the Ski Bowl was open, Everitt Memorial Highway was regularly plowed its full 14-mile length, enabling year-round access to Sargents Ridge and many excellent cross-country and ski-mountaineering routes. Now the road is plowed only as far as Bunny Flat, and the remaining 3 miles to Panther Meadow and the Ski Bowl are left to thaw on their own, usually by the end of June.

From the Ski Bowl parking lot, a maze of old dirt service roads winds upward through a cirque to the location of the old top terminal at 9,200 feet, where several radiotelephone antennae remain. From this location, head directly north until intersecting Green Butte Ridge, the southern margin of vast Avalanche Gulch. Follow the ridge to a gap just north of Point 9,572, then contour left to the traditional route (Route 1) near Helen Lake. Because the last 3 miles of Everitt Memorial Highway aren't plowed, access to this route is seldom open until late June or early July. By then, long stretches of exposed scree and talus are on the climbing route. Descend your route of ascent.

Variation 2 Green Butte Ridge to Sargents Ridge (Route 3)

➤ See map, p. ix

DIFFICULTY: D2
TIME: 1+ days

Instead of traversing left to the traditional John Muir route, continue climbing Green Butte Ridge until it joins Sargents Ridge at 12,000 feet. Follow Sargents Ridge (Route 3) to its juncture with the traditional route (Route 1) at Thumb Rock. Descend via the climbing route.

ROUTE 3 Sargents Ridge ➤ See map, p. ix

DIFFICULTY: D2
ACCESS: Everitt Memorial Highway via Old Ski Bowl (N41° 21.717' W122° 12.033')
CAMPSITES: Panther Meadow, Old Ski Bowl lodge parking area
TIME: 1+ days

Named for John Sargent, a forest ranger who enjoyed climbing Mount Shasta in the 1940s, this ridge is an excellent winter route because of its general lack of avalanche exposure. Summer popularity has waned in recent years because late openings of the last 3 miles of Everitt Memorial Highway have prevented easy access. By mid- to late summer, lack of snow on the route makes for some unpleasant climbing over talus and scree. In winter and spring, however, this is a high-quality route worth the effort to ski or snowshoe from Bunny Flat to a base camp in the old Mt. Shasta Ski Bowl.

From any of several good campsites in the Ski Bowl cirque, climb northeast on gentle shoulders that join the ridge proper. A good landmark on the crest above is Shastarama Point (Point 11,135), a major, turreted crag. Beyond this large outcrop, the ridge flattens for 0.25 mile. Here you'll have excellent views of the Mud Creek and Konwakiton Glaciers, as well as the impressive, precipitous depths of Mud Creek canyon. Continue upward on the steepening ridge, avoiding obstacles and exposure by bearing left. Join Route 1 at the Red Banks–Thumb Rock saddle and follow it to the summit.

Descend the climbing route or Route 1 to the Ski Bowl traverse (Route 2).

Variation 3 Traverse to Mud Creek Glacier ➤ See map, p. ix
DIFFICULTY: D2
TIME: 1 day

From the long, flat ridge just beyond Shastarama Point, a short traverse to the east takes you to the small Mud Creek Glacier.

This glacier has a stark, alpine beauty but is seldom visited. There is also a beautiful hidden lake behind Shastarama Point. Descend via the approach route.

ROUTE 4 Green Butte Ridge ➤ See map, p. ix
DIFFICULTY: D1–D2
ACCESS: Everitt Memorial Highway via Bunny Flat (N41º 21.233' W122º 13.967')
CAMPSITE: Bunny Flat
TIME: 1+ days

This route and the Old Ski Bowl route (Route 2) share a distinction: while not particularly aesthetic or notable, these routes are popular among climbers with limited time because one can start climbing right from a parking lot and avoid hiking into a base camp. Green Butte Ridge is popular as an accessible winter route safe from avalanche exposure.

From the parking area at Bunny Flat, climb northeast on gentle, forested slopes until you're above timberline and level with Green Butte, the large, rounded shoulder at 9,200 feet that juts out to the south. Continue northeast on Green Butte Ridge to join the Sargents Ridge route (Route 3), or traverse to the traditional route (Route 1) as in the Old Ski Bowl (Route 2) route description.

Descend via the climbing route.

ROUTE 5 Casaval Ridge ➤ See map, p. ix

DIFFICULTY: D2–D3
ACCESS: Everitt Memorial Highway via Bunny Flat (N41º 21.233' W122º 13.967')
CAMPSITES: Horse Camp, Sand Flat, Bunny Flat
TIME: 2–2+ days

Casaval Ridge is the striking, cockscomb-like ridge north of Avalanche Gulch. Worldly mountaineers compare it to famous classics of the Alps. The route offers an excellent winter ascent and an airy, stimulating spring and early-summer climb. Ample bivvy sites add to the attraction of the climb. After early summer the route is not recommended due to lack of snow and much loose rock.

From the Sierra Club Foundation cabin at Horse Camp, a broad toe of the ridge is only a few hundred yards north. Climb this wide ridge to about 9,800 feet, where it makes a jog to the left at an excellent bivvy site and joins serrated Casaval Ridge proper. The first part of the ridge is fairly low angle; you can go around towers blocking the way on either side, but left (north) is usually easier. The ridge begins to steepen at 10,800 feet, a little above Helen Lake, which is visible to the right (south). This part of the ridge, called the first window, offers escape to Helen Lake via moderate slopes on the right. Though the route steepens here, there are many wide sections.

A second escape, the second window, occurs at 11,800 feet. Here, another broad, moderate slope curves down into Avalanche Gulch above Helen Lake. (During times of avalanche danger, it's unwise to descend into main Avalanche Gulch.) A few short, steep sections are on the ridge at 13,000 feet. This route joins Route 1 at 13,500 feet and continues to the summit.

Descend either the climbing route or one of the Avalanche Gulch routes as time and conditions dictate.

Variation 5 The West Face ➤ See map, p. ix

DIFFICULTY: D2
ACCESS: Everitt Memorial Highway via Bunny Flat (N41° 21.233' W122° 13.967')
CAMPSITES: Horse Camp, Sand Flat, Bunny Flat, Hidden Valley
TIME: 1–2 days

North of Casaval Ridge is an aesthetic, long, shallow gully that begins in Hidden Valley at 9,700 feet and ends nearly 4,000 feet later at the broad snowfield at the base of Misery Hill. This route retains snow long into summer and is an excellent alternative route when Casaval Ridge is too rocky and devoid of snow to be pleasant or safe.

It is best to begin the climb from a high camp in Hidden Valley. From the Sierra Club Foundation cabin at Horse Camp, traverse and gradually climb north. Cross several gullies until you reach Hidden Valley at 9,200 feet. A good landmark to aim for from the cabin is a spire of rock (Point 9,487) that coincides closely with true north. Once you reach the ridge below and west of the spire, you can descend easily into Hidden Valley, an extensive flat basin that makes an excellent, well-protected high camp. When the gully begins to narrow at its top, stay left of the dark orange palisades—the westernmost volcanic flow of the Red Banks.

You can choose to reach the West Face gully from the lower stretches of Casaval Ridge, where you must traverse north to reach the gully. Descend either the route of ascent or Cascade Gulch (Route 6).

ROUTE 6 Cascade Gulch ➤ See map, p. xi

DIFFICULTY: D1–D2
ACCESS: Everitt Memorial Highway via Bunny Flat (N41° 21.233' W122° 13.967')
CAMPSITES: Bunny Flat, Sand Flat, Horse Camp, Hidden Valley
TIME: 1–2 days

The famous geologist Clarence King, who is credited with discovering the glaciers on Mount Shasta (the first glaciers to be officially identified in the United States), made one of the first ascents of this route in 1870. Clarence King Lake, within Shastina's crater, was named after him.

From the Sierra Club Foundation cabin at Horse Camp, traverse and gradually climb north. Cross several gullies until you reach Hidden Valley at 9,200 feet, using the same approach for the West Face. From there, stay left of the main watercourse—and the waterfall at the head of Hidden Valley—and climb to the 12,000-foot saddle between Shasta and Shastina.

From the saddle, climb east along Shasta's wide west ridge, avoiding some steep drop-offs onto the Whitney Glacier. As the ridge narrows, follow the narrow snowfield above the Whitney Glacier bergschrund to a point atop the Red Banks and a little west of Misery Hill. Be prepared for short sections of roped climbing if it's necessary to cross the bergschrund.

You can avoid glacier travel by following the serrated upper ridge west of the Whitney Glacier. Very careful route finding, generally climbing toward the southwest, is necessary to avoid some short, steep sections. Depending on seasonal conditions, a rope may be necessary here. Join Route 1 and continue to the summit.

Variation 6a Ascent of Shastina ▶ See map, p. ix
DIFFICULTY: D1
TIME: 1 day

From the Shasta–Shastina saddle a short scramble leads west to Shastina's summit pinnacle. Shastina's crater is more than 0.5 mile across and several hundred feet deep. Clarence King Lake looks like a turquoise jewel when it becomes free of snow midsummer.

Variation 6b Upper Whitney Glacier to Summit ▶ See map, p. xi
DIFFICULTY: D2–D3
TIME: 2 days

The upper Whitney Glacier is very smooth compared to the chaotic middle and lower parts of the glacier and offers pleasant climbing with few crevasses. From the Shasta–Shastina saddle, ascend Shasta's west ridge a few hundred feet until the easiest entry to the glacier presents itself. Usually several snowfields spill over onto the glacier from the ridge, providing convenient access. Avoid descending directly from the saddle to the glacier, as a bergschrund and icy cliffs can be dangerous.

If you climb too high on the west ridge, some short rock faces prevent easy entry to the glacier. Once on the glacier, climb, curving east, and follow rock ribs to the summit plateau. Descend either the climbing route or Shasta's west ridge to Cascade Gulch (Route 6).

Shastina to the Hotlum–Bolam Ridge

Many shallow gullies exist from Diller Canyon clockwise around Shastina to the Whitney Glacier. The climbing is generally arduous because of large amounts of talus and loose rock. Diller Canyon is often climbed in conjunction with a ski descent, but in times of little snow, loose 4th class rock makes the last 1,000 feet undesirable.

ROUTE 7 Whitney Glacier ➤ See map, p. xii
DIFFICULTY: D2–D3
ACCESS: North Gate Trailhead (N41° 28.117' W122° 10.367')
CAMPSITES: Whitney, Bolam, unnamed intermittent creeks
TIME: 2+ days

The Whitney Glacier was named for Professor Josiah D. Whitney, the leader of the California Geological Survey and of the scientific exploration of Mount Shasta in 1862. It is California's longest glacier, stretching almost 2 miles, and its foot is covered with an enormous quantity of rubble and debris.

A base camp on the lower glacier is an experience for the senses: with the towering flanks of Shastina rising more than 4,000 feet to the west and the long, broad Whitney–Bolam Ridge bordering the cavernous canyon on the east, the tableau looks like the Alaska Range or the Himalayas. In early evening's shadows or by moonlight, the scale and the vastness of the scene seem totally different from their daytime aspects. Add to this the constant creaking and grinding of the glacial ice, the irregular sounds of water, and the cannonades and crescendos of rockfalls and breaking seracs (pinnacles of ice)—all contribute to a dramatic alpine setting.

From the North Gate road access, there are many base camp choices. In winter or early spring, you can approach easily on skis, with several comfortable benches for base camp. In summer, it's usually best to set up base camp on the flat lower glacier. There are also some miniature meadows and springs near timberline just west of the glacier terminus, but these can be difficult to find.

Climbing the lower glacier is relatively straightforward, but there might be minor route-finding problems in late summer and fall as crevasses begin to open. Avoid venturing close to Shastina's flanks because of the threat of rockfall, and be wary of a similar threat from the upper slopes of Shasta. The center of the lower glacier is generally safest.

When snow still covers most of the glacier, the big icefall adjacent to the Shasta–Shastina saddle is the only major obstacle along the route.

In early season several paths may become visible, but the glacial geography is an ever-changing kaleidoscope in three dimensions, and you must be prepared to use your best skills and judgment to improvise a route.

In late summer and fall, the enormity of the open crevasses and the bergschrund spanning the glacier's full width, as well as the precariousness of the seracs, make the icefall a much more serious undertaking. By then, acres of seracs have toppled and avalanched, mostly during the heat of midsummer days. Either side of this icefall section can offer reasonably safe passage. The east side is a little more direct; the west side offers the sanctuary of the Shasta–Shastina saddle but can be steeper in places. Above the icefall, follow the smooth upper glacier to the summit plateau.

Descend the climbing route.

Variation 7a Whitney Icefall for Serac and Ice Climbing

➤ See map, p. xi
DIFFICULTY: D3
TIME: 2+ days

When ice conditions are at their best, the main icefall is a worthy objective for ice-climbing practice. There is sufficient ice most of the time except in midwinter, when the icefall is covered with snow. In summer warm temperatures can create extremely unstable conditions within the icefall. Seracs (pinnacles of ice) can topple at any time, and it's recommended to stay away.

Variation 7b Whitney–Bolam Ridge ➤ See map, p. xii
DIFFICULTY: D1–D2
TIME: 1–2 days

This seldom-done variation is very nice when there is sufficient snowpack; without the snowpack, it's an unenjoyable trudge through loose talus. This ridge can provide a quicker descent to base camp than the Whitney Glacier itself, and in times of adequate snow it is an outstanding ski descent route. The route may be done in its entirety, or you

The Summit Monument

Alice Cousins astride Jump-Up on the summit

Ed Stuhl Collection

In the 1870s the U.S. Coast and Geodetic Survey decided that it was necessary to increase the accuracy of its maps. Signal stations were planned for the summits of Mount Shasta, Mount Saint Helena (near Clearlake, California), and Mount Lola (west of Reno, Nevada) to be included as part of the survey grid. On April 30, 1875, John Muir and local guide Jerome Fay climbed Shasta to take barometric measurements and study the feasibility of placing a tower on the summit. A fierce storm caught the pair on the summit, and, unable to descend, they spent the night huddled over the summit's hot sulfur fumaroles. Muir's account of the experience, "Snow-Storm on Mount Shasta," is one of his most famous writings.

can traverse east from the Whitney Glacier onto the ridge to avoid the Whitney icefall.

From base camp the route appears as a series of gentle shoulders arranged like ascending steps. Follow the path of least resistance over the steps; bearing southwest is usually easiest. At about 12,000 feet, the steps give way to a continuous slope that can be followed to the summit plateau. Descend the ascent route.

The signal station, with a nickel-plated copper top, was fabricated in San Francisco and carried in pieces to the summit, where it was assembled and anchored in place. In the summer of 1878, U.S. Coast and Geodetic Survey assistant Benjamin Colonna spent nine continuous days on Shasta's summit waiting for favorable conditions. Finally, on August 1, Colonna exchanged flashes with surveyors on the other two peaks. The line from Mount Shasta to Mount Saint Helena, 192 miles, was the longest terrestrial distance ever measured, surpassing the previous record of 169 miles from Spain across the Mediterranean to Algeria.

After the survey work was completed, the monument was abandoned for any further scientific use. In fact, it became adorned with graffiti as climbers scratched and painted their names on the tower.

In 1903 guide Tom Watson led Alice Cousins astride horse Jump-Up to the summit via the Clear Creek route (Route 15). It was the first horse to reach Shasta's pinnacle, and the picture of them next to the signal station was used in "Ripley's Believe It Or Not" features for many years. Then, in the winter of 1903, the monument collapsed, a victim of Shasta's severe winds and weather. The crushed cylinder can still be seen at the south base of the summit pinnacle. The copper reflector was brought down in 1946 and is on display at the Mt. Shasta Sisson Museum in the town of Mt. Shasta.

ROUTE 8 West Bolam Glacier ➤ See map, p. xiii
DIFFICULTY: D2
ACCESS: North Gate Trailhead (N41° 28.117' W122° 10.367')
CAMPSITES: Bolam Creek, numerous morainal steps and benches
TIME: 1–2 days

The Bolam Glacier is very broad and smooth, excellent for newcomers to glacier climbing or as a first glacier climb on Mount Shasta. The routes are general, and several variations are possible. You can also escape, if necessary, to the wide ridge to the west at several points. Major difficulties on the upper glacier include a long, obvious bergschrund and some small crevasses.

The Whitney Glacier base camps can position you for the climb, but it's more advantageous to traverse higher under the Bolam Glacier to a campsite on one of the many morainal shelves. Climb the broad west side of the glacier, passing two very large rock islands on their right sides. From steeper slopes on the glacier's upper reaches, you can attain the summit plateau via mixed climbing to the west or good, short gullies to the east.

Descend the climbing route.

ROUTE 9 East Bolam Glacier ➤ See map, p. xiii
DIFFICULTY: D2
ACCESS: North Gate Trailhead (N41° 28.117' W122° 10.367')
CAMPSITES: North Gate, surrounding forest. The many flat and sandy lateral moraines between the Hotlum and Bolam Glaciers also offer excellent campsites and numerous sources of water.
TIME: 1–2 days

When the North Gate road is open, often by mid- to late June, it offers the best access to the Bolam Glacier. The approach hike or ski is moderate,

At the Bolam Glacier camping area

and all of the base camps are comfortable. Choose one of the many exceptional high camps described in Route 10 and traverse to the glacier from the vicinity of 10,000 feet. You can also continue west from North Gate, past very large, descending benches, to the jumbled moraines at the glacier's foot. Climb to the west of the two large rock islands, and from there follow Route 8 to the summit. Descend the climbing route.

Variation 9 Bolam Gully ➤ See map, p. xiii
DIFFICULTY: D3
TIME: 1–2 days

Climb the long, shallow gully left (east) of the two large rock islands described in the two previous routes. The snow in this gully is usually in excellent condition, though it can sometimes be icy. When above the second rock island, you can bear right and follow steep mixed climbing to the summit area, or else traverse east to Route 10 and follow that path to the summit. Descend either the climbing route or Route 10, depending on conditions and time.

ROUTE 10 Hotlum–Bolam Ridge ➤ See map, p. xiv
DIFFICULTY: D2
ACCESS: North Gate Trailhead (N41° 28.117' W122° 10.367')
CAMPSITES: North Gate, surrounding forest. The many flat and sandy lateral moraines between the Hotlum and Bolam Glaciers also offer excellent campsites and numerous sources of water.
TIME: 1–2 days

The Hotlum–Bolam Ridge route is truly a path for all seasons. The access road takes you to an unexpectedly high elevation. The trail through North Gate and the surrounding forest is pleasant, and campsites are numerous with water close at hand. In winter, when parts of the mountain's north side experience a rain shadow, road access reaches high enough to enable a fairly direct and gentle ski or snowshoe ascent to a suitable base camp. The most difficult season for this route is often late summer and fall, when it regularly becomes quite icy. In general, the ridge is not prone to avalanche danger.

Ascend the trail through the North Gate area, the shallow ravine between a large mesalike lava flow on the left (east) and large, rugged outcrops on the right (west). Several base camp choices are possible. In early summer, when there is still sufficient snow on the north slopes of the mesa, it can be easily ascended. The top of this formation is a descending series of broad, sandy benches protected from weather that usually offer summerlong water in shallow gullies from many accumulated snowdrifts. These benches at about 9,500 feet provide some of the most comfortable above-timberline camping anywhere on Shasta.

The Exploration and Naming of Shasta's Glaciers

From the cover of Up and Down California in 1860–1864 by William H. Brewer via Wikimedia Commons

The 1864 California Geological Survey Field Party: James T. Gardiner, Richard D. Cotter, William H. Brewer, and Clarence King

A decade after the 1849 California gold rush, Josiah Whitney was appointed as state geologist and was bestowed the task of completing a geological survey with special attention to mineral resources. Whitney's assistant was William Brewer. In 1862 they followed the Sacramento River north to Mount Shasta, climbing the peak on September 12 and obtaining barometric readings at the summit to compute an elevation of 14,442 feet. At the time, it was considered the highest point in the United States.

After the climb, Brewer wrote a letter to an old friend, George Jarvis Brush, professor of metallurgy at Yale University, describing his adventures on Shasta. One of Brush's students, Clarence King, happened by the office and read Brewer's letter. For King, who eventually rose to the directorship of the U.S. Geological Survey, this was a pivotal moment. He immediately volunteered as an assistant field geologist to Whitney's California survey.

In late summer, when the mesa's north slopes are devoid of snow, loose talus and scree make a direct ascent to the mesa's top very unpleasant. In that season, continue around the mesa's west shoulder, gain elevation, and cut back to the left (east) on wide talus ramps to a point midway on the series of benches atop the formation. You can also camp a short distance west of the mesa near an unnamed all-season stream, or

While doing fieldwork on Shasta's slopes in 1864, King and Brewer discovered an unusual milky-looking stream, suspiciously similar to the silty runoff from a glacier. King inquired, and Brewer replied that he had climbed the peak without discovering any glaciers. This was a time when geologists were debating the role of glaciers in America. Evidence of an ancient glacial epoch in North America had been recognized, and climbers had been on Cascade glaciers farther north, but American geologists and glaciologists believed that no active glaciers remained in the United States.

King returned to Mount Shasta in the fall of 1870 as director of the government-sponsored Geologic Exploration of the Fortieth Parallel. When King and his assistants climbed Mount Shasta in September 1870, they ascended via the huge saddle between Shasta and Shastina and were rewarded with their first views of an active glacier in the United States. Shasta's great northside "ice river" was later named for King's mentor, Josiah Whitney. King later told Brewer, "That stream haunted me for years, until I got on Mount Shasta and found the glaciers." The discovery was considered one of the most important geologic events of the decade.

The credit for naming Shasta's other glaciers belongs to the famous Western explorer Major John Wesley Powell. Powell was a brilliant scholar who wrote more than two dozen dictionaries of American Indian languages and dialects. In 1879 he came to Northern California to study the Wintun tribe and climbed Mount Shasta on November 1 of that year. Afterward, he named Shasta's four other major glaciers with Wintun words in honor of the tribe: Hotlum ("steep rock"), Bolam ("big" or "great"), Konwakiton ("muddy"), and Wintun (the tribal name). The names were inscribed in official records maintained by the U.S. Board on Geographic Names in 1897.

continue up past a lovely, small waterfall to excellent campsites between 9,000 and 10,000 feet.

The climbing route follows broad snow slopes toward the obvious Hotlum–Bolam Ridge. If you bear right, you'll find that it's steep, but you'll gain the ridge quickly. In good snow conditions it's better to contour left, skirt the bergschrund and crevasse hazards on the Hotlum's west lobe, and then follow a broad snow ramp that angles up and to the right to a large, flat platform at 12,800 feet on the ridge. If the lower ridge and the broad ramp are icy, you can traverse left on snowfields that skirt the west side of the middle Hotlum Glacier, then curve around and up to the platform at 12,800 feet. Be prepared for roped glacier travel if you plan to venture onto the Hotlum Glacier. From the platform, the imposing Hotlum headwall looms to the left in full view.

Follow a triangular snowfield leading up the ridge to the west toward two obvious rock towers, or "ears," which can be seen from well down the mountain and which are good points of reference. Pass these towers on the right and climb through large broken blocks on the ridge. Follow the ridge to the summit. If wind or ice makes the uppermost ridge undesirable, you can continue past the two ears on their right, pass through any of several notches on the ridge, and ascend an easy snow gully hidden on the ridge's west side. This gully can be followed until several short, shallow ribs offer easy return to the ridge just short of the summit. You can also continue climbing in the gully to the hot springs beneath the summit pinnacle. In late summer and fall, large sections of this route can become icy. Descend the climbing route.

Variation 10 Side Trip to the Chicago Glacier from the North

➤ See map, p. xiv

DIFFICULTY: D1–D2

TIME: 1 day

From base camp atop the mesa, ascend a few hundred vertical feet and traverse southeast to this seldom-visited and isolated glacier.

North and Northeast Sides: Hotlum and Wintun Glaciers

ROUTE 11 Hotlum Glacier ➤ See map, p. xiv

DIFFICULTY: D3
ACCESS: Brewer Creek Trailhead (N41° 26.100' W122° 7.967')
CAMPSITES: Brewer Creek, Gravel Creek, moraine lakes and meadows
TIME: 2 days

From an impressive rock headwall beginning at nearly 13,000 feet, the Hotlum Glacier descends in a gentle S-turn through three spectacular icefalls. At the lowest icefall—a huge broken and convoluted formation just to the right (north) of a prominent rock prow—the glacier levels out and ends in several acres of fascinating ice ribs. Spread out below this terminus are rugged morainal hummocks and small, hidden lakes. Finally, the headwaters of Gravel Creek and other smaller streams emerge into the red fir and hemlock forests below.

Several fine base camp areas are found in the Brewer and Gravel Creek drainages, from which the glacier may be climbed to one of the summit variations. You can also establish a high camp on a prominent rock prow at 11,700 feet below and north of the middle icefall. In spring and early summer the glacier is predominantly smooth from accumulated snow. In late summer and fall, the curved path of the Hotlum Glacier becomes a maze of crevasses, and careful route finding is necessary. At this time the icefalls also come into their best condition for serac climbing.

The climbing route ascends to the right (north) of the lower icefall, then gradually curves upward and left (south) of the middle icefall. Continue upward, again gradually bearing right (north), until you reach the broad upper glacier, which is slightly below and to the left of the upper icefall. At this point, though the slope remains moderate, several crevasses may extend completely across the glacier. In late summer and in times of diminished snow, these abysses can halt easy upward progress. The ridge to the left (south), which becomes most evident above the lower icefall, offers an escape at several points. You can then follow this ridge to the summit.

The usual, challenging finish is to climb the steep, often icy couloirs just left of the headwall to an area atop the headwall and just northeast of the summit pinnacle. From most points on the middle and upper reaches of the Hotlum Glacier, you can also traverse right (north) to join Route 10, the Hotlum-Bolam Ridge route. Descend the climbing route or Route 10.

Variation 11a Hotlum Glacier Headwall ➤ See map, p. xiv
DIFFICULTY: D3+
TIME: 2 days

From the bergschrund, climb increasingly steep snow to the very apex of the glacier beneath the rock headwall. Three to five rock pitches (some class 5.8), depending on route finding, lead to easier climbing just below the summit pinnacle. The combination of exposure, some loose rock, required commitment, and high altitude make this one of the most difficult routes on the mountain.

Variation 11b Hotlum Headwall Ice Gully ➤ See map, p. xiv
DIFFICULTY: D3+ mixed climbing (rock and ice) up to very difficult
TIME: 2 days

Just right (north) of the obvious headwall in Variation 11a is one of Shasta's longest, steepest ice gullies. In the fall, hard water ice abounds, and this gully is one of the best ice climbs on Mount Shasta. In summer, scattered snow patches can thinly cover parts of the ice to create deceptively safe but actually very dangerous conditions. The route is easy to follow but is steep, and it ends at easier climbing below the summit pinnacle.

Variation 11c Hotlum Icefalls ➤ See map, p. xiv
DIFFICULTY: D3
TIME: 2 days

The three Hotlum icefalls offer Shasta's best and most accessible serac climbing. A careful choice of your base camp or high camp will enable you to enjoy exceptional ice climbing only minutes from your tent. The lower icefall, situated at the front of the huge Hotlum amphitheater, conveys a feeling of grandeur, and its mazes of seracs are exciting to explore. In addition, the broad and gentle terminus below the lower icefall is great for beginning glacier and ice training. Plan your high-camp location and climbing activities very carefully, because seracs on the middle and lower icefalls may weaken and collapse, especially during warm weather.

Route 11: Hotlum Glacier

Variation 11d Side Trip to the Chicago Glacier from the South

➤ See map, p. xiv

DIFFICULTY: D1–D2
TIME: 1 day

From any of the base camps for the preceding Hotlum Glacier climbing routes, you can traverse north about 0.5 mile with little gain or loss in elevation to the Chicago Glacier. Seldom visited, this glacier received long-term scientific attention and study by the University of Chicago's Department of Geophysical Sciences because of its apparent growth during the late 20th century. You can also reach the glacier by a gentle traverse over talus from where the whitebark pine flats meet the undulating morainal hills in the vicinity of Gravel Creek.

ROUTE 12 Hotlum–Wintun Ridge ➤ See map, p. xvi

DIFFICULTY: D2
ACCESS: Brewer Creek Trailhead (N41° 26.100' W122° 7.967')
CAMPSITES: Brewer Creek, Gravel Creek, moraine lakes and meadows
TIME: 1+ days

This fine route is one of the most scenic on Shasta's east side, and it's a great alternative to the often-crowded Avalanche Gulch climbs. The first ascent was likely made by Norman Clyde in September 1935. If the route is followed correctly, almost no glacier technicalities will be encountered. The name *ridge* is a slight misnomer as most of the route follows broad, permanent snowfields located between the Hotlum and the Wintun Glaciers. Above 12,400 feet, the ridge separating the glaciers becomes very distinct, and it is one of the variations to the summit.

The Brewer Creek meadows at timberline make an excellent base camp and offer a very direct start to the climb. Follow the snowfield in the main drainage upward, climbing left (south) of the lower Hotlum icefall and rock cliffs, where developing crevasses could be troublesome. Continue upward to 12,400 feet, where the ridge becomes distinct. From this high point, choose one of the following summit variations.

Variation 12a Traverse Left (South)   ➤ See map, p. xiv
DIFFICULTY: D2
TIME: 1+ days

Traverse left (south) to the upper snowfields at the right (north) side of the Wintun Glacier. Pass a solitary, triangular rock island, and then climb back to the right and upward to the rock palisades descending from the summit area. Follow the cliff line to the left (west) until you encounter the summit snowfield. Curve around to the north to ascend the summit pinnacle. When there is abundant, stable snow on the route, this variation is safe, direct, and enjoyable. If there is ice, bad visibility, or concern about nearby crevasses, consider the next variation.

Variation 12b Rock Ridge Direct   ➤ See map, p. xiv
DIFFICULTY: D2
TIME: 1+ days

Climb directly up the Hotlum–Wintun rock ridge that begins at 12,400 feet. With careful route finding, the ridge is 3rd class. If 4th class sections are encountered, they are usually very short and avoidable by traversing to easier climbing. Ice, verglas (a thin film of ice covering rocks), or bad weather will make a rope advisable. The ridge ends almost directly at the summit.

Variation 12c Traverse Right (North)   ➤ See map, p. xiv
DIFFICULTY: D2–D3
TIME: 1+ days

This third alternative angles right (north) at the ridge break at 12,400 feet and follows a steep snowfield that skirts the left side of the Hotlum headwall. As this snowfield-cum-gully narrows, stay left of a thin rock rib and climb to easy ground at the summit area.

Descending the Eastside Routes

An eastside descent is potentially hazardous for unexpected drop-offs, and consideration should be given to all the variables. Generally, what you have just climbed is fresh and familiar in your mind, and for this reason it should be the descent of choice.

If key features and landmarks are noted on the ascent, they can be very useful during the descent. If snow conditions change, visibility or weather worsens, or darkness falls, the two snow variations (Variation 12a and Variation 12c) can become very dangerous with unexpected drop-offs and/or crevasses not far from the safe route. Wands or flagging should be placed at critical points on the ascent to mark the route. The rock ridge (Variation 12b), though slower going than the snow variations, avoids any serious drop-offs. At 12,400 feet, continue the descent on the broad snowfield.

ROUTE 13 Wintun Glacier ➤ See map, p. xvi
DIFFICULTY: D2–D3
ACCESS: Brewer Creek Trailhead (N41° 26.100' W122° 7.967')
CAMPSITES: Brewer Creek, Gravel Creek, moraine lakes and meadows
TIME: 1+ days

The Wintun Glacier, named for a local American Indian tribe, has many different sections. The upper glacier is wide and clean, and from a beginning just below the east face of the summit pinnacle, the east tongue of the glacier descends smoothly to plateaus between Brewer and Ash Creeks. The southeast tongue of the glacier pours over a precipitous icefall and into steep Ash Creek canyon. The lower glacier is an interesting maze of crisscrossing crevasses, and the icefall offers fine practice climbing.

You can establish a base camp near Brewer Creek or one closer to the glacier by traversing south to the highest of three flat hills seen silhouetted on the ridge south of Brewer Creek. From these hills, you can see most of the route, and a descending traverse will take you to the lower glacier. Except for spring and early summer, some talus will be encountered on this traverse—try to scout ahead to avoid the loosest sections. Pass the icefall on either side, depending on snow conditions and where the least debris from above appears to be falling. Easier climbing on the left side of the glacier leads to the summit snowfield. Descend the climbing route or Wintun Ridge (Route 14).

Route 13: Wintun Glacier

Variation 13a Traverse to Wintun Ridge ➤ See map, p. xv
DIFFICULTY: D2
TIME: 1+ days

If conditions on the lower Wintun Glacier and the icefall appear unstable, or if debris is raining down from above, you can traverse south out of the canyon to Wintun Ridge. Climb on the broad ridge to the summit snowfield, or traverse to the upper Wintun Glacier and follow it to the summit.

Descend the climbing route.

Variation 13b Brewer Creek Approach to the Wintun Glacier
➤ See map, p. xv
DIFFICULTY: D2
TIME: 1+ days

Using this approach you can avoid the lower Wintun Glacier and its icefall entirely, while gaining the easier middle and upper reaches of the glacier. From the Brewer Creek drainage, follow snowfields upward and to the south. Attain the broad, eastern tongue of the Wintun Glacier and follow it to the upper glacier and the summit snowfield.

ROUTE 14 Wintun Ridge ➤ See map, p. xvi
DIFFICULTY: D1–D2
ACCESS: Clear Creek Trailhead (N41º 21.967' W122º 7.517') or Brewer Creek Trailhead (longer; N41º 26.100' W122º 7.967')
CAMPSITES: Clear Creek, Pilgrim Creek's many intermittent meadows and springs
TIME: 1 day

This ridge is relatively moderate, has excellent views, and, during the right conditions, offers a superb ski descent as fine as any on Mount Shasta. From a base camp above Clear Creek, Cold Creek, or Pilgrim Creek, climb the wide, lower ridge by the best snowfields. The middle and upper sections of the route are generally clean and smooth, but avoid drop-offs to either side of the ridge, as well as a small, south tongue of the Wintun Glacier. Attain the summit snowfield at its southeast end and follow it to the summit pinnacle. Descend the climbing route.

Variation 14 Side Trip to Watkins Glacier See map, p. xvi
DIFFICULTY: D1–D2
TIME: 1 day

From the 11,000-foot area on Wintun Ridge, a short southward traverse brings you to the Watkins Glacier. This small glacier and cirque are beautiful, and the detour is well worth the time.

East and Southeast Sides: Clear Creek, Mud Creek Canyon, and Konwakiton Glacier

The southeast side of Mount Shasta is distinguished by a very broad, gentle shoulder between the Konwakiton Glacier and the great cleft of Mud Creek canyon, and the Wintun Glacier. This gradual slope was noticed early in Shasta's climbing history, and it became popular because of its moderate slope. This was the way Jump-Up, the first horse to stand atop Mount Shasta, made his notable climb in 1903. Evidence of an old trail is often seen in times of light snow. High camps of early climbers are still found, occasionally complete with neat, small stacks of sun-bleached firewood carried above timberline before the advent of today's ultralight campstoves.

ROUTE 15 Clear Creek See map, p. xvi
DIFFICULTY: D1
ACCESS: Clear Creek Trailhead (N41° 21.967' W122° 7.517')
CAMPSITES: Clear Creek, Pilgrim Creek's many intermittent meadows and springs
TIME: 1 day

From one of several excellent base camp sites between Mud Creek and Clear Creek, the broad, gradual slope of the climbing route is very evident, resembling a gently tilted isosceles triangle. In spring and early summer, abundant snow allows an easy climb. However, the southern exposure causes the snowpack to melt rapidly, leaving unpleasant talus and scree. In late summer you will need to try to find a route that links snowfields together to bypass most of the talus. At 13,000 feet avoid steep chutes dropping off on either side of the climbing route to the Konwakiton and Wintun Glaciers. This pleasing route ends on the broad summit snowfield just west of the summit pinnacle. Descend via the climbing route.

ROUTE 16 Konwakiton Glacier from the East ➤ See map, p. xvi
DIFFICULTY: D3
ACCESS: Clear Creek Trailhead (N41° 21.967' W122° 7.517')
CAMPSITES: Clear Creek, Pilgrim Creek's many intermittent meadows and springs
TIME: 1+ to 2 days

The Konwakiton ("muddy one," in the Wintun Indian language) Glacier is one of Shasta's smallest glaciers, extending down only to about 12,000 feet. The glacier lies at the head of Mount Shasta's most immense gorge, Mud Creek canyon, and only the imagination can ponder the scale of the geologic and glacial events that shaped this huge chasm. Here is some of the steepest and most rugged—and potentially riskiest—terrain on Mount Shasta.

Route 16: Konwakiton Glacier

The best approach to the climbing route is via a traverse from the Clear Creek route (Route 15). Begin the traverse at an elevation near or above waterfalls emanating from the glacier's foot. Rockfall can be a serious problem on this route. Take great care on the approach, as the sun can soften the rock's frozen mortar from above. A very steep rock ridge divides the glacier; you can pass left of this ridge to gain immediate entrance to the steep icefall, or pass the ridge on its right to avoid the icefall altogether. There are many variations on the glacier—from steep, difficult ice to challenging mixed climbing on rock ribs. The slope of the glacier decreases near its apex. Climb northeast to the summit snowfield and continue to the summit pinnacle. Descend via the Clear Creek route.

ROUTE 17 Konwakiton Glacier from the South ➤ See map, p. xvi
DIFFICULTY: D3
ACCESS: Everitt Memorial Highway via Old Ski Bowl (N41° 21.717' W122° 12.033')
CAMPSITES: Panther Meadow, Old Ski Bowl lodge parking area
TIME: 1–2 days

From Sargents Ridge you can establish a high camp on the north side of Shastarama Point (Point 11,135) or at the base of the small Mud Creek Glacier. Approach the Konwakiton Glacier from the southwest. Current conditions will dictate the best approach. You can avoid the icefall by climbing steep gullies on the left. When adequate snow cover is present and loose rocks are cemented well in place, it's convenient to traverse below the icefall to direct ascent lines east of the rock ridge dividing the glacier. Descend via Sargents Ridge.

Skiing down Route 10: Hotlum–Bolam Ridge

SKIING, SNOWBOARDING, AND SKI TOURING

Vast glaciers and snowfields, immense vertical relief, and plentiful winter snowfall have long attracted skiers and snowboarders to Mount Shasta. Indeed, one popular backcountry ski magazine has referred to Mount Shasta as the "best corn skiing on planet Earth!" In winter, skiers and snowboarders of all abilities, as well as snowshoers and winter campers, can find endless opportunities for recreation on the mountain. Even during the height of a storm, enjoyable skiing and snowboarding await within the protected forests below timberline. In spring and early summer, many of the climbing routes can be combined with an exciting partial or complete descent on skis or snowboard—beginning from as high as the summit. Favorable snow conditions often allow descents of more than 6,000 vertical feet!

At the beginning of the 20th century, skis were used almost exclusively for transportation, not recreation. But some early pioneers discovered adventure and fun on the downhill runs. In the 1930s skiers flocked to Snowman's Hill on Mount Shasta's gentle southern slopes to schuss and watch ski jumping contests among some of North America's finest skiers. Southern Pacific Railroad had special weekend trains from San

Francisco to this popular ski destination. Historic Snowman's Hill still remains a U.S. Forest Service–maintained snow-play area.

The earliest ski descents of Mount Shasta were made in the 1920s and 1930s, remarkable events considering the archaic equipment of the time, as well as the magnitude and steepness of the mountain. In 1925 Swiss mountaineers skied as far as the saddle between Shasta and Shastina. In the 1930s a group of Yale ski team members, intimidated by Mount Shasta's scale, estimated that "The drop from the summit to Horse Camp can be done easily, by an experienced man, in 5 minutes!"

Snowman's Hill, circa 1943

In April 1932 Halvor Halstad, Steffan Trogstad, and Ted Rex, professional ski jumpers who came to Mount Shasta to compete at Snowman's Hill, made the first ski descent from Shasta's summit in 1 hour and 15 minutes. For fun they made a small ski hill and jumped over the cabin at Horse Camp! The first solo ski descent was made by ski coach Otto Steiner in 1936. Today, skiers and snowboarders come from afar for Mount Shasta's world-class descents and ski touring.

In this chapter we describe the range of skiing and snowboarding possibilities on Mount Shasta. Ski mountaineering and backcountry skiing require knowledge of technique, proper equipment, and the ability to be self-sufficient. Preparation for and experience with various snow conditions, weather conditions, and avalanche dangers should be considered de rigueur, as there are no formulas or shortcuts for avoiding potential dangers and hazards on Mount Shasta—or on any other mountain. Though several Shasta glaciers offer moderate descents, they still require proper glacier travel technique, ability, and equipment.

The most crucial hazard that backcountry skiers and snowboarders have to contend with is an avalanche. Beginners who stick to meadows and gentle slopes in the forest have little to worry about, but when you enter the realm of backcountry skiing, ski mountaineering, and snowboarding, you enter the realm of potential avalanches. Avalanche forecasting is a fascinating subject, and we urge you to seek instruction. Many excellent texts on the subject are available, as are classes, seminars, and avalanche-transceiver training. Because Mount Shasta receives plenty of snowfall, most (but not all) avalanches on Shasta are direct-action avalanches, which occur during or soon after storms as a result of new snow loading the slopes.

Current snow and weather conditions can be obtained locally to help you plan and prepare for an outing. Phone numbers for 24-hour weather and climbing information, as well as informative websites, are listed on page 24; shastaavalanche.org has daily posts.

Ski and snowboard routes can be described only in general terms. Terrain, snow conditions, weather, visibility, and potential avalanche danger vary seasonally, and even daily. Certain routes and tours are best at certain seasons, as indicated below.

Skiing and snowboarding on Mount Shasta may be divided into four general categories:

1. A ski or snowboard descent in conjunction with one of the climbing routes. This may be the conclusion of a summit climb, or skiing and snowboarding may be the objective.

2. Highway winter access. The best access for beginner/intermediate skiers and snowboarders, as well as access to some selected

advanced runs, is Everitt Memorial Highway on Shasta's southwest side. This highway is regularly plowed as far as Bunny Flat.

3. Ski-in base camps. Many excellent skiing areas require a long skiing approach, but a base camp in a wilderness setting makes the effort worthwhile. Access to such places via gravel roads varies with the season.

4. Lift-serviced and cross-country ski areas. Mt. Shasta Ski Park and Nordic Center both operate on a regular schedule throughout the winter.

In addition, we describe:

5. Castle Lake highway access, Mount Eddy, and the west side of Strawberry Valley.

6. Mount Shasta ski circumnavigation.

Early skiers on Mount Shasta *(Mt. Shasta Collection, College of the Siskiyous)*

Skiing and Snowboarding: The Climbing Routes

Many of the climbing routes on Shasta are also excellent ski routes. With a little added equipment and preparation, these climbing routes can become exciting ski or snowboard descents. Access, route descriptions, and other information appear in detail in the Climbing Routes chapter. The following is a sequential listing—clockwise around Mount Shasta from Avalanche Gulch—of the best climb/ski routes, along with special comments as they apply.

Key to Ski and Snowboard Routes

SEASON   The time of year for the best skiing and snowboarding of the route or area.

LEVEL   Degree of difficulty of skiing in area. (We've tried to balance the ratings among cross-country/Telemark, snowboard, and downhill equipment. On the more difficult descents, the skiing tends to be a little harder than the rating if you're using cross-country gear and a little easier if you're using randonee or downhill gear.)

   Indicates previously recorded avalanche activity.

ROUTE 1 John Muir (Avalanche Gulch)
SEASON: Spring–early summer
LEVEL: Advanced

Avalanche Gulch, the immense, open bowl on Shasta's southwest flank, offers nearly unlimited skiing possibilities. For those desiring a descent from the actual summit, this route has the most consistent snow conditions, though the reaches above the Red Banks often have poor quality and/or sparse snow cover, as well as icy sections. Choose your line carefully through or around the Red Banks, as this series of chimneys can be difficult to negotiate; there is no dishonor in taking the board(s) off here. The skiing and boarding are best on corn or spring snow.

Variation 1a ⚠ Left of Heart

SEASON: Spring–early summer
LEVEL: Advanced–expert

This steep variation avoids the Red Banks when they're lacking enough skiable snow, and for pure exposure this run is one of the most exciting on Mount Shasta. The Red Banks headwall varies seasonally, but you can expect pitches up to and exceeding 40 degrees.

ROUTE 2 Old Ski Bowl

SEASON: Spring–early summer
LEVEL: Intermediate–advanced

This bowl is pleasant and scenic. It's impractical to ski this route starting from above 10,000 feet because of steep rock cliffs, but the route can be connected by traverse to Route 1 for maximum vertical drop. Snowmobiles are allowed in this area and are not uncommon.

ROUTE 4 ⚠ Green Butte Ridge

SEASON: Late winter–early spring
LEVEL: Intermediate–advanced

This ridge offers access to several other bowls and can also be connected to Route 1. If you're itching to get above treeline but conditions are avalanche-prone, this route often has a much lower hazard.

Variation 5 ⚠ The West Face

SEASON: Spring–early summer
LEVEL: Advanced–expert

This steep, open gully is a candidate for the extreme category, but sun-softened spring snow can bring it into the range of many skiers. The run includes a continuous fall line shot of 4,000 feet, making it one of Mount Shasta's most exciting descents. The upper headwall can be steep, but moving west lessens the severity of this short section.

ROUTE 6 ⚠ Cascade Gulch

SEASON: Spring–early summer
LEVEL: Intermediate–advanced

This very delightful, curving, open bowl allows a moderate, traversing descent from Shastina to Horse Camp.

ROUTE 7 ⚠ Whitney Glacier

SEASON: Late winter–early summer
LEVEL: Intermediate–advanced

With adequate snow cover, the vast lower glacier is excellent for skiing, and it provides access for winter and spring ascents of the upper glacier.

Variation 7b ⚠ Whitney–Bolam Ridge

SEASON: Late winter–early spring
LEVEL: Advanced

This ridge is an excellent ski descent when there is ample snow.

ROUTE 8 ⚠ Bolam Glacier from the Northwest

SEASON: Late winter–early spring
LEVEL: Intermediate–advanced

The Bolam's lack of serious crevasses makes it Shasta's best glacier to ski.

ROUTE 9 ⚠ Bolam Glacier from the Northeast

SEASON: Late winter–early summer
LEVEL: Intermediate–advanced

The North Gate road and trailhead, often open by late spring, make this one of the earliest-opening ski descents apart from the south side.

Variation 9a ⚠ Bolam Gully

SEASON: Spring
LEVEL: Advanced–expert

The Bolam Gully is another ski descent route in the extreme category.

ROUTE 10 ⚠ Hotlum–Bolam Ridge
SEASON: Spring–early summer
LEVEL: Advanced

Above 13,000 feet the ridge itself may not be skiable because of exposed rocks and wind-scoured snow and ice, but the snowfields on either side of the ridge remain in skiable condition remarkably late into summer and can be connected in many ways for superb ski descents.

ROUTE 11 ⚠ Hotlum Glacier
SEASON: Spring
LEVEL: Advanced

The Hotlum Glacier is not especially steep, but it can be difficult to ski because of the large icefalls and a maze of crevasses. However, careful route finding will provide excellent ski terrain.

ROUTE 12 ⚠ Hotlum–Wintun Ridge
SEASON: Late winter–early summer
LEVEL: Intermediate–advanced

This route is considered by many to be one of the finest descents on Mount Shasta. It is usually one of the longest-lasting snow slopes on the mountain, often skiable through the summer or until sun cups become too large. During favorable snow conditions, it is possible to ski off the summit via this route and Route 13, the Wintun Glacier.

The upper sections can be steep with wind-scoured snow, but the eastern exposure often produces excellent corn snow. Minimal crevasse hazard makes for a very enjoyable and consistent descent. The roads to the trailhead are usually inaccessible until early or mid-June, depending on the winter snowpack, but this descent is worthy of an early ski-in approach.

Route 10: Hotlum–Bolam Ridge

ROUTE 13 ⚠ Wintun Glacier
SEASON: Spring–early summer
LEVEL: Advanced

The upper reaches of the glacier offer excellent skiing and can be connected with Route 12 for a long descent.

ROUTE 14 ⚠ Wintun Ridge
SEASON: Late winter–spring
LEVEL: Intermediate–advanced

This route is a spring favorite, offering broad, wide skiing terrain with moderate slopes.

ROUTE 15 ⚠ Clear Creek
SEASON: Late winter–spring
LEVEL: Intermediate–advanced

This route is another spring favorite, also offering broad, wide skiing terrain with moderate slopes.

Winter Access: Everitt Memorial Highway

Siskiyou County road crews plow Everitt Memorial Highway only to the 11-mile point at Bunny Flat. The remaining 3 miles of road remain beneath snow, usually through June, but the road is still easy to follow, and it makes for an enjoyable ski tour.

Everitt Memorial Highway provides access to some of the finest and most varied skiing found anywhere on Shasta. Parking is available at Bunny Flat (11 miles), Sand Flat (10 miles), and the Wagon Camp turnout, or the switchback (7 miles). Snowmobiles are allowed below Everitt Memorial Highway up to the Old Ski Bowl. They are also allowed in the Ski Bowl basin. Always use caution when these vehicles are nearby or when sharing a narrow track with them.

The following areas are described in descending progression, from higher to lower elevation, along Everitt Memorial Highway, starting from the Old Ski Bowl and continuing clockwise along the highway around the mountain.

Unplowed Everitt Highway, Bunny Flat to Old Ski Bowl
LEVEL: Beginner–intermediate
OTHER ACTIVITY: Snowshoeing

The gently contoured Everitt Memorial Highway, covered by snow its last 3 miles, from Bunny Flat to Panther Meadow, is easy to follow as it winds through stately Shasta red fir trees. This is an excellent short tour with an easy return.

Old Ski Bowl
LEVEL: Intermediate–advanced

In the days of the old ski area, the two sides of this large, open cirque were identified as the West Bowl and the East Bowl. The West Bowl, adjacent to precipitous Green Butte, is steep and challenging; the East Bowl is more rolling and gentle.

Tour to South Gate Meadows
LEVEL: Intermediate–advanced
OTHER ACTIVITY: Snow camping

From the bottom of the Ski Bowl cirque, traverse east through an obvious notch in Sargents Ridge. Continue through The Gate, the pass between Red Butte and the mountain, and into the beautiful hemlock forests of South Gate Meadows. Continue to ski farther east for outstanding winter views of the Konwakiton Glacier and Mud Creek canyon.

Panther Meadow
LEVEL: Beginner–intermediate
OTHER ACTIVITIES: Snowshoeing, snow camping

Below the Old Ski Bowl and just west of Gray Butte are the gentle rolling hills and forest of Panther Meadow. Close proximity to parking at Bunny Flat makes the meadows a desirable destination for snow camping or ski touring. A pleasant side trip, all downhill, is to ski 2.5 miles cross-country south to Mt. Shasta Ski Park. Prearrange a shuttle or a pick-up for this variation.

Wagon Camp
LEVEL: Intermediate

From Panther Meadow traverse west, parallel to and below Everitt Memorial Highway, through forest and open slopes. Finish at the Wagon Camp switchback, a convenient shuttle point.

Gray Butte Northwest Face ⚠
LEVEL: Advanced

Gray Butte is the steep hill bordering the southeast edge of Panther Meadow. The best approach to ski the north face of the butte is via the ridge on the left (north) of the north face.

Powder Bowl and Sun Bowl ⚠
LEVEL: Intermediate–advanced

Powder Bowl and Sun Bowl are the two very distinct, above-timberline bowls between Green Butte and Bunny Flat; Sun Bowl is the western-most. The easiest approach is via Green Butte Ridge from Bunny Flat. The lower parts of these bowls may be reached from several points along the unplowed Everitt Memorial Highway track. These two bowls offer some of the finest early spring snow on Shasta, as long as avalanche risk is minimal.

Broadway ⚠
LEVEL: Intermediate–advanced

The wide lower half of Green Butte Ridge is called Broadway. The skiing here is excellent when sufficient snow covers some very large rocks.

Bunny Flat Area
LEVEL: Beginner–intermediate
OTHER ACTIVITIES: Snowshoeing, snow camping

Bunny Flat, at the end of the plowed part of Everitt Memorial Highway, is a parking area, staging area, and hub for ski tours in every direction.

The most popular half-day ski tour on Mount Shasta is undoubtedly the short jaunt to the Sierra Club Foundation cabin at Horse Camp. From Bunny Flat head north a few hundred yards, passing through an obvious break in the near ridge to the west, then gradually climb northwest. Yellow metal triangles—old license plates—on trees mark this ski trail. A 25-foot metal tower, used by the U.S. Forest Service as a rain-collecting gauge, marks the two-thirds point of the route. The cabin is always unlocked, and it makes a wonderful winter base camp or a place for lunch and socializing.

You can also ski to Sand Flat or Wagon Camp from Bunny Flat, shuttle back up Everitt Memorial Highway, and repeat the run.

Horse Camp Area and Beyond ⚠️

LEVEL: Beginner–advanced
OTHER ACTIVITIES: Snowshoeing, snow camping

The Sierra Club Foundation cabin is an excellent base camp for skiing in the cabin's own backyard: the immense Avalanche Gulch basin. North of the cabin are advanced-level bowls, Cascade Gulch and Hidden Valley.

Horse Camp to McBride Springs ⚠️

LEVEL: Intermediate–advanced

This is one of the best descents on the southwest slope of Shasta. From the Sierra Club Foundation cabin, traverse north 0.25 mile and follow the slopes on the south side of Cascade Gulch until you meet Everitt Memorial Highway near the McBride Springs Campground. This ski descent is more than 4 miles long and drops more than 4,000 vertical feet.

Sand Flat Area

LEVEL: Beginner–intermediate
OTHER ACTIVITIES: Snowshoeing, snow camping

Sand Flat is a beautiful open meadow with postcard-perfect views of upper Mount Shasta. The meadow can be reached by a 0.5-mile ski-in on one of two easy-to-follow snow-covered roads. There is a parking area at the upper road (10.2 milepost and SAND FLAT sign), and another at the lower road, about 0.6 mile down Everitt Memorial Highway from Upper Sand Flat Road and its parking area. The upper road is nearly flat; the lower one is steeper but more fun to ski down. The U.S. Forest Service has placed signs on the trees to mark several easy scenic tours within the area. A cross-country ski-trail map for Sand Flat is available at the Mt. Shasta Ranger Station.

Red Fir Flat
LEVEL: Beginner
OTHER ACTIVITIES: Snowshoeing, snow camping

Located just below the lower road to Sand Flat, the gentle terrain of Red Fir Flat is especially suited for beginners.

SPECIAL EXTRA: Diller Canyon

SEASON: Spring–summer ⚠
LEVEL: Advanced–expert

Diller Canyon is the very large and unmistakable cleft in the west face of Shastina. It was named after U.S. Geological Survey geologist Joseph Diller, who conducted studies on Shasta in the 1880s. Throughout the winter, strong jet-stream-velocity north winds carry enormous quantities of snow from Shastina's flanks to the lee (south) side of the canyon, where it remains throughout the summer. Though this is not a particularly worthy climbing route, as a ski descent, it is one of the longest and most exciting on Shasta. For the expert skier, this one should not be missed. And for snowboarders, consider this the largest and longest half-pipe on the planet!

Access to Diller Canyon can be a problem because of rough dirt roads; a truck with ample clearance or a four-wheel-drive vehicle is necessary. Drive up Everitt Memorial Highway 2.7 miles to a dirt road on the left marked BLACK BUTTE TRAILHEAD. Follow this dirt road 0.8 mile, then turn east on another dirt road. Follow this road as it curves north, then east, then north again to as high as possible along Shastina's flank. (Disrepair and constant additions to this maze of logging roads cause yearly changes to access direction. If in doubt, follow the line of least resistance to as high as possible; the hike to Diller Canyon is scenic and not very long.)

Ski-In Base Camps: Wilderness Skiing

Skiing into a plateau or a protected valley, establishing a comfortable base camp, and then skiing untracked terrain during this most magical time in the wilderness creates a true winter delight. Mount Shasta has several such secret spots; the only limiting factor is your imagination. A guidebook may be useful, but a sense of adventure is the key. A little extra effort may be required to get to the chosen areas, but the reward is wilderness skiing at its finest. Following are a few of the best areas.

The north and northeast sides of Shasta sometimes experience unusual winter weather effects: a cold stillness descends and dry powder snow remains in the valleys and the gullies for weeks on end. When the Military Pass Road is open, you can access the North Gate and the Inconstance, Gravel, and Brewer Creek drainages. Excellent snow is usually found here.

Similar outstanding snow conditions can often be found on Shasta's east flanks, but access depends on how far you can first drive up Pilgrim Creek Road. A long ski-in to base camp is usually necessary, but the terrain is gentle. The Cold, Pilgrim, Ash, and Clear Creek drainages offer the best snow.

Lift-Serviced and Commercial Ski Areas

Mount Shasta has a long history of downhill skiing, going back to the early 1930s when the Mount Shasta Snowmen ski club was organized. Snowman's Hill, at the crest of CA 89 between the towns of McCloud and Mt. Shasta, featured a 100-meter ski jump considered one of the best ski jumping hills in North America in the 1930s. Southern Pacific Railroad had special weekend trains from the San Francisco Bay area to Snowman's Hill, and several ski jumping championships were held there. The U.S. Forest Service still maintains this area for snow play, sliding, and sledding.

When Everitt Memorial Highway was completed in 1940, several plans were proposed for ski lifts on the mountain. These different proposals included, at various times, lifts from the town of Mt. Shasta to the top of the mountain! Mt. Shasta Ski Bowl, located above Panther Meadow, operated 1958–1978. Mt. Shasta Ski Park, below Panther Meadow and Gray Butte, opened in 1985. It has three triple chairs and a surface lift, complete lodge facilities, and a ski school, and it also offers night skiing—all on groomed trails serving beginners to experts. In addition, it has a Telemark program and instruction and a Nordic ski area with more than 40 kilometers (25 miles) of groomed trails, lodge facilities, and lessons.

The Eddys, Castle Lake, and Beyond

The Eddys refer to the mountains across the valley to the west of Mount Shasta, dominated by 9,025-foot Mount Eddy. The Klamath, Siskiyou, and Scott Mountains all meet in this area, which is very old geologically compared to Mount Shasta. For the adventurous, hidden backcountry bowls with spectacular scenery and possibilities for exploration abound in the Eddys. Castle Lake Road, snowplowed as far as the lake on an irregular basis, is a good departure point. A special backcountry ski touring map for this area is available at The Fifth Season outdoors shop in Mt. Shasta; other maps are available at the ranger station.

Mount Shasta Ski Circumnavigation

Mount Shasta's quintessential ski tour is for advanced and expert backcountry skiers. The general rule of thumb is to remain near timberline, though many variations are possible.

A clockwise direction of travel is best, usually starting from the Sierra Club Foundation cabin at Horse Camp. Starting clockwise from here gets you to Shastina's northwest flanks relatively soon, where it's not uncommon to find that high winds have scoured the slopes dry of snow. If the slopes are devoid of snow, this starting point allows skiers to easily backtrack to the cabin. Skiers may want to use binoculars from near Weed to scout the conditions on Shastina before embarking on their journey.

A counterclockwise course could bring you to the northwest side of Shastina several days after beginning the trip, with no convenient escape route if lack of snow prevented a skiing return to the cabin. Some additional caveats: You can cross Ash Creek canyon either above or below the falls. Going above the falls entails elevation gain but offers an easy canyon crossing. Going low offers the protection of the forest but a steeper canyon to cross. Mud Creek canyon should be crossed in the vicinity of its confluence with Clear Creek. Any higher crossing is steeper and longer; a lower crossing means additional gorges to contend with and considerable elevation to regain. Avalanche activity has been recorded throughout the circumnavigation route.

This circumnavigation is an unforgettable ski trip on a great mountain. Needless to say, careful preparations, heavy-duty equipment, and self-sufficiency are necessary. Plan on four or five days for the ski circumnavigation of Mount Shasta.

HIKING AND CLIMBER ACCESS

Hiking on Mount Shasta is pleasant and breathtaking. Four good trails access the mountain's southern, eastern, and northern flanks, and all of them climb a couple of miles through forests of tall conifers framing vistas of the peak above and surrounding territories below. All these trails deliver you to the uplifting openness of Shasta at treeline and to high-country camping and climbing routes. While similar in this basic pattern, each trail has a different character and leads to different opportunities for adventurous side trips. A fifth popular trail on the southeast side of Shasta traverses to an area of classically scenic alpine and subalpine meadows. Another more remote but still-worthy trail leads to Whitney Falls. All trails except Whitney Falls can serve for day hiking, for backpacking in to camp, or as climber access. We present them here counterclockwise.

Finally, if you're up for a great adventure, we encourage you to consider the magnificent, demanding immersion in Mount Shasta, the cross-country backpack tour around the mountain (see page 99).

Wilderness Permits and Regulations

All of Shasta's trails enter the Mt. Shasta Wilderness, where a permit is required and dogs are not allowed. All of the trailheads have stations providing self-service, no-charge permit forms for you to fill out and carry. Cross-country travel is allowed, but if you are striking off-trail, be ready to navigate your own way, and please tread carefully to avoid the plants that struggle to live on Shasta's volcanic slopes. Damp, meadowy areas and dry, sandy areas are both easily trampled and ruined. When you camp, please find already cleared sites at least 100 feet from water and trails. There is precious little firewood at most elevations within the wilderness area, so no campfires are allowed—you must cook on a stove. It's also not allowed to cache equipment or supplies, except, of course, while you are hiking or climbing away from your campsite.

All areas on Mount Shasta are special and fragile, and to keep them that way it's required to pack out not only your trash but also your fecal waste. Special bags for this are available at the trailheads. Carryout is easier and more sanitary if you package these bags inside something fairly bombproof, for example, a bear canister or a river-runner's dry bag. When you return to the trailhead, deposit your bags in the red containers at the vault toilets there. This policy has really helped keep Mount Shasta a great mountain to climb and explore.

Dispersed camping is allowed in the Shasta-Trinity National Forest, including at the trailheads. But if you are camping outside of a wilderness permit jurisdiction, you need to go by the ranger station in town to obtain a camping permit (also no charge) and to learn about fire safety, current fire conditions, and possible restrictions.

Climbing Regulations

Climbing fees on Mount Shasta have been authorized under the Federal Lands Recreation Enhancement Program of 2005. All climbers going over 10,000 feet need to purchase a Summit Pass. These cost $25 per person and are valid for three days. Self-service fee envelopes are available at the trailheads, where you'll need either a check or exact change. If you're climbing the mountain more than once during a calendar year, you can get an annual Summit Pass for $30 from the ranger stations in downtown Mt. Shasta and McCloud. Citizens and permanent US residents age 62 or older who possess a Golden Age Passport get a 50% discount on these fees. The collected fees go toward the general recreation operations of Shasta-Trinity National Forest, including the salaries of the climbing rangers, who do an excellent job of educating climbers and cleaning up after thoughtless individuals. Nevertheless, the program remains controversial for taxing mountaineering differently than other recreation within the national forests.

Trailheads

To access the trails on Mount Shasta, you'll need a car. The most popular trails await on the southern side of the mountain, reached by an easy drive along the paved Everitt Memorial Highway. The trails on the east and north sides of the peak are at the end of backcountry dirt roads that are a bit rough and not maintained. None require four-wheel-drive vehicles in theory, but high clearance is recommended. Low-clearance sedans sometimes cannot make it and are not recommended. These routes weave through a maze of logging roads, and we depend on U.S. Forest Service signs to point the way. Logging operations and, in rare cases, washouts occasionally prompt the U.S. Forest Service to reroute access to these trailheads, but the agency does a much better job of keeping the signs current than maintaining the roads. For current road conditions to a specific trailhead, call the local ranger stations at 530-926-4511 or 530-964-2184.

The following driving directions begin at the stoplight intersection in downtown Mt. Shasta, at Lake Street and Mt. Shasta Boulevard. At that intersection you'll find a public tap issuing wonderful Shasta water to fill your canteens. For each trailhead we list elevations and latitude and longitude as an aid to those who might need help from a GPS device for returning to the car.

South Gate Meadows

Bunny Flat and Old Ski Bowl Trailheads

Everitt Memorial Highway leads to the **Bunny Flat** and **Old Ski Bowl Trailheads**, where the trails to **Horse Camp** and **South Gate Meadows** begin.

From downtown, drive northeast on Lake Street, which soon veers left and continues north as Washington Drive. Pass the high school and rise on a steady grade into open land on the lowest slopes of the mountain. About 3 miles from downtown, the highway curves right, and at the curve you'll notice a sign pointing out the dirt road that leads to another interesting hiking trail, to the 6,325-foot-high summit of Black Butte, the prominent, subsidiary volcanic cone just to the west. Continue on the Everitt Memorial Highway as it curves right, and you'll climb steadily through a couple of switchbacks. At mile marker 11, you'll reach the Bunny Flat Trailhead (6,950'; N41° 21.233' W122° 13.967').

On busy days scores of cars may be parked at Bunny Flat. Dispersed bivouac camping is allowed in this vicinity, though there is no water.

To reach the **South Gate Meadows Trail**, keep driving up the Everitt Memorial Highway past Bunny Flat another 3 miles, climbing a few broad switchbacks to road's end at the **Old Ski Bowl** trailhead (7,840'; N41° 21.717' W122° 12.033').

Sand Flat Alternative Trailhead

An alternative trail connects to the Horse Camp Trail, starting at Sand Flat (6,800'; N41° 21.233' W122° 14.984'). Most people prefer to hike in from Bunny Flat, but some will start from Sand Flat, particularly during some snowy seasons when the Everitt Memorial Highway is not plowed all the way to Bunny Flat. The dirt-road turnoff onto Sand Flat Road is a bit past mile marker 10 on the highway, 0.75 mile before Bunny Flat. The trail begins at the dirt road's end, climbs through an old clear-cut, and proceeds to meet the main Horse Camp Trail after about 0.75 mile.

The Story of the Everitt Memorial Highway

In 1912 residents decided to promote Shasta tourism by putting in a wide trail to Horse Camp from Sisson—the name for the town until 1922, when it was renamed Mt. Shasta. The road would be labeled the Mt. Shasta Snowline Highway. Work finally began in the late 1920s, before it was ever passable to wagons and when it had become clear that it would need to be a motor road. During a summer of construction a fire broke out on Shasta's southern flanks, and on August 25, 1934, the supervisor of the Shasta National Forest, John Samuel Everitt, was killed fighting that fire. The roadway was renamed in his honor, and in 1940 it was completed all the way to Panther Meadow. In 1956 the road was paved. During the heyday of the Mt. Shasta Ski Bowl, the entire highway was kept open year-round, but with the closing of the lifts in 1978, Siskiyou County began plowing only up to Bunny Flat.

Clear Creek and Brewer Creek Trailheads

Clear Creek and **Brewer Creek Trailheads** are at the ends of forest roads on the east side of Shasta. Each is an hour's drive or more from town; Clear Creek is closer. Begin by heading southeast on Mt. Shasta Boulevard, and stay on this main street as it veers south out of the downtown area. In 2 miles, the road curves over I-5 and becomes CA 89, going east. Proceed on CA 89 over Snowman's Summit, through the hamlet of McCloud. Go 13.2 miles on CA 89; you'll see a prominent sign reading MT. SHASTA WILDERNESS TRAILHEADS pointing left to Pilgrim Creek Road. Turn here and continue north across railroad tracks into the forestland east of the mountain. In 5.3 miles (as of 2017) from CA 89, you'll see the turn left to **Clear Creek Trailhead**. Follow signs as you drive northwest on rough dirt roads about 9 more miles to reach the trailhead (6,520'; N41° 21.967' W122° 7.517').

To reach the **Brewer Creek Trailhead**, continue on Pilgrim Creek Road (past the Clear Creek turnoff), and in 7.1 miles from CA 89, turn left (north) on Military Pass Road (Forest Service Road 43N19), where you'll see signs pointing left for Brewer Creek. Follow these signs about

12–15 more miles to the trailhead, depending on current U.S. Forest Service signage (7,280'; N41° 26.100' W122° 7.967').

North Gate Trailhead

To reach **North Gate Trailhead** you'll drive around the west side of Mount Shasta. This will take at least an hour, and the last 0.75 mile is rough. From downtown, drive south down Lake Street 0.5 mile, and get onto I-5 heading north. After 8.2 miles take Exit 747 for the town of Weed. Turn right onto Weed Boulevard/Volcanic Legacy Scenic Byway, and at the second stoplight keep right to stay on US 97 N. After 14.9 miles from I-5, keep an eye out and turn right (east) onto Military Pass Road. A historical marker here commemorates this road as a pioneer settlers' wagon train route. Continue on this primary dirt road, crossing under railroad tracks, and follow signs that eventually point the way south, 8.7 miles to the trailhead (7,000'; N41° 28.117' W122° 10.367').

Whitney Falls Trailhead

Shasta's most obscure trailhead gives access to a fascinating destination. In recent years outburst floods from the Whitney Glacier have damaged the dirt road (and in fact closed US 97 at times), but as of this writing the route has been reworked and is quite passable. From downtown Mt. Shasta, follow the directions as per the North Gate Trailhead to US 97 N in Weed. At 12.1 miles from I-5, turn right onto the unsigned Bolam Road. If you come to paved County Road A12, which branches north (left), you've gone 0.3 mile too far on US 97. On fairly good-quality Bolam Road, keep driving south, avoiding an eastbound (left) road at 0.2 mile from US 97 and another 0.8 mile farther. Another 0.5 mile farther, continue straight across railroad tracks and maintain a southbound course past a couple of other forks to reach the end of the road, 3.7 miles from US 97 (5,466'; N41° 28.933' W122° 14.517').

Trail Descriptions

TRIP 1 Horse Camp Trail
DISTANCE AND DIFFICULTY: 3.4 miles round-trip, moderate

The best-known trail on Shasta takes you to the timberline cabin owned by the Sierra Club Foundation. The cabin is the starting point

Trail to Horse Camp

for the most popular ascent route on Shasta, Avalanche Gulch. With Shasta rising directly above the cabin and a fountain of pure spring water piped to it, Horse Camp lures many hikers to stay overnight at one of the established camp spots there. See the directions on page 86 to Bunny Flat Trailhead.

Description

With a full view of Mount Shasta, the trail (an old road for the first 0.75 mile) starts north along the west edge of an expansive dry meadow. Then it promptly turns west over a low ridge, heading northwest through other open areas of Bloomer's rabbitbush, on the fringes of Shasta red fir forest. The wide trail jogs north, then continues climbing gently to a broad, open ravine where young red firs lie strewn about. These trees were victims of the large snow avalanches that roar down Avalanche Gulch during heavy winters.

From this ravine the trail turns northwest up the side of a wooded ridge to reach the trail coming up from Sand Flat. This latter trail has pretty much followed this ridge from the forested Sand Flat trailhead, climbing through a manzanita clearing with logging stumps and then through forest again to this junction. Most people prefer the higher, more scenic start from Bunny Flat.

Now you hike on a steady grade northeast along the flank of the ridge, pausing perhaps to hear the twitters and calls of mountain chickadees, as well as the squawks and reprimands of Clark's nutcrackers and Steller's jays. At the end of the climb a jog northwest heralds your arrival at the arid meadows of Horse Camp. Here the Sierra Club Foundation posts a summer caretaker who can answer questions about everything from climbing conditions to the cabin's history, from the latest local environmental controversy to where it's best to camp. The foundation charges a small fee (currently $5 per tent) to camp in the Horse Camp area. There is also an innovative composting toilet. Anyone may visit the cabin and use its library. Camping is allowed inside the cabin only in emergencies and in winter.

Horse Camp is so named because it was here that early-day climbers tethered and hobbled their horses while ascending Shasta. The front side of the cabin looks out to the Trinity Alps, and from the back side you can scout the slopes of Shasta. Above Horse Camp the fir forest gives way to open timberline slopes, luring hikers farther. Behind the cabin you'll find (Mac) Olberman's Causeway, a line of broad, flat stones (that Olberman brought and installed using a big rock bar) that starts climbers up the traditional climbing route to the summit. This path makes a nice extension for hikers to follow a short way as well.

Cross-Country Side Trips from Horse Camp

Side Trip 1a Hidden Valley
DISTANCE AND DIFFICULTY: 2.5 miles round-trip, difficult

Between Shasta and Shastina runs the major drainage called Cascade Gulch, and at about 9,300 feet within that gulch sits a broad bench called Hidden Valley. Hidden Valley provides vistas south over seemingly all of California, and it's an excellent high camp area for climbing both Shasta and Shastina. There is a distinct, if rough, track to get up there, and a sign at the lodge points in its direction to get you started. This is not a maintained trail though, and it won't hurt to orient yourself before you start. From the cabin look along the left skyline of Shasta, at a compass bearing almost due north, and you'll see a small but striking rock pinnacle. Hidden Valley lies immediately on the other side of that pinnacle. Allow a good 1–2 hours from Horse Camp.

Strike off toward the pinnacle and then climb sandy, forested slopes to a tiny basin. Continue north, climbing past a few outstanding tall firs and up more sandy slopes. The route traverses in and around little ridges and ravines to eventually turn into the drainage of Cascade Gulch. The final stretch to Hidden Valley is an exasperating, traversing climb up a rocky slope to the head of the gulch and Hidden Valley. Once there you're rewarded with a mostly reliable stream in a krummholz "forest." Here Shasta and Shastina loom over you in an amphitheater of high mountain grandeur.

Side Trip 1b Green Butte
DISTANCE AND DIFFICULTY: 3.0 miles round-trip, moderate

This is a modest adventure to a panoramic high point not quite 2 miles from Horse Camp. From Horse Camp you can identify the butte as the high point almost due east, with distinctive greenish rock that's steeper on its right (south) side.

From Horse Camp hike east across the sandy, open drainage of Avalanche Gulch and then start climbing steadily, aiming for the broad, relatively gentle slope in the major ridge to the east. This slope has escaped the action of glaciers that have flowed down Avalanche Gulch. From this broad slope, hike northeast to crest the ridge near a less prominent high point, then turn southeast to descend along the very narrow, rocky ridge crest to the summit of Green Butte. Many of the summit rocks are fulgurites, rocks fused into glassiness by lightning strikes. From here you can enjoy a great panorama, including the Old Ski Bowl and Sargents Ridge farther east.

South Gate Meadows

TRIP 2 South Gate Meadows Trail
DISTANCE AND DIFFICULTY: 4.4 miles round-trip, moderate

This popular tour leads to lush green meadows surrounded by groves of delicate mountain hemlock.

Begin at the Old Ski Bowl trailhead.

On some maps this area is still labeled as Squaw Valley, but out of respect to retire the old Algonquian vulgarity, the new official name is used here.

From the trailhead at the Everitt Memorial Highway's last switchback, start off east-northeast and climb over a gap in the low ridge ahead. The trail continues southeast into a stark, silent basin where moppyheaded pasqueflowers and hardy little shrubs like knotweed and buckwheat grow in stark isolation. The track veers northeast to climb through The Gate (also known as South Gate), the gap between Red Butte and Mount Shasta. Continue straight through the gap and then take a short, steep drop into the wooded canyon below. Now the trail steadily descends into hemlock country, keeping north above the rocky canyon floor. Before long the track turns northeast through a hemlock grove to a stream. You cross another fork or two of the stream and then climb a short way to arrive at upper South Gate Meadows. Here sedges, heather, and many wildflowers grow in a rich carpet beside a perennial brook, fed by a spring that issues from the snowy ramparts of Shasta above. At most drainages on Shasta, water percolates deep and out of reach, but the substrate underlying South Gate Creek somehow keeps a steady flow at the surface, feeding "stringer" meadows like this one well into the forest belt. These meadows—so precious on Shasta—are easily trampled into mud, so please refrain from hiking on them. If you are camping in this area, please find a site in the forest away from the fragile green carpet.

TRIP 3 Clear Creek Trail
DISTANCE AND DIFFICULTY: 4.9 miles round-trip, moderate

A short hike on this trail takes you to spectacular vistas along the rim of Mud Creek canyon. Then it leads to timberline, where panoramas include Shasta's four eastern glaciers, and access opens to popular eastside climbing routes.

The Clear Creek Trail evolved from an old jeep road pushed through by four-wheel-drive enthusiasts and woodcutters. Since the designation of the Mt. Shasta Wilderness (1984), the U.S. Forest Service has blocked the jeep track and constructed a well-graded hiking path.

Description

The hike starts in a smooth furrow and rises gradually under venerable red firs hung with lime-colored staghorn lichen. A few lazy switchbacks let you enjoy this sylvan enclosure for not quite a mile, then deliver you to the east rim of Mud Creek canyon at about 6,900 feet. This is a memorable panorama, as the canyon drops from your feet in steep slopes of cinders and andesite, and you can hear and see the powerful churn of the creek 500–600 feet below. Up on Shasta's left skyline you see Shastarama Point and Thumb Rock above the Konwakiton Glacier. The Mud Creek Glacier gathers its dwindling mass from a small basin hidden behind Shastarama. At the head of the canyon the Konwakiton Glacier hangs broken and steep amid andesite cliffs and debris slopes. This is a menacing headwall, and climbers (who venture up from the Old Ski Bowl) would do well to consider the message of this view. Mud Creek issues out of these two small glaciers and plummets through the canyon over two powerful waterfalls. Farther right, on Shasta's eastern flanks, are the Watkins and Wintun Glaciers.

Mud Creek canyon is Shasta's largest and oldest canyon, dating from the proto–Mount Shasta of 300,000 years ago. During snowy epochs glaciers have filled the canyon, transporting debris and helping to excavate its grand depths. During warm spells in the 1920s and 1930s, the Mud Creek Glacier steadily disintegrated and issued outburst floods. These spilled out of the canyon, blocked the railroad near McCloud, and muddied the Sacramento River past Redding.

Resuming the hike, you stay near the canyon edge, climbing gradually on a roller coaster forest course. As you reach the area above the confluence of Clear Creek and Mud Creek far below, you leave most of the firs behind and enter whitebark pine country, where Clark's nutcrackers squawk at your entry into their domain. You can follow the track into the krummholz zone to near 8,300 feet. At this height Clear Creek's drainage broadens and allows one to traverse west 0.25 mile to a surprisingly verdant destination, the meadowy source springs of Clear Creek. Campsites can be found here, some of which date to climbers in the late 1800s. If you do camp, please find the most established site you can, and protect the water sources from both trampling and contamination.

TRIP 4 Brewer Creek Trail
DISTANCE AND DIFFICULTY: 4.0 miles round-trip, moderate

Constructed in 1986, this trail offers well-graded access to timberline on Shasta's less-visited east slopes. The hike rewards you with pleasant walking through unusual forests of whitebark pines (which frame good views of Shasta and its glaciers), access to summer ski slopes, and some of Shasta's best glacier climbing.

You start hiking south 0.25 mile and then jog west before resuming a southern course. Half a mile from the trailhead you start a series of long, lazy switchbacks that take you from an open red fir forest into a parkland of whitebark pines. Hardy wildflowers, including violets, phlox, and Shasta knotweed, dot the ashy soil between trees.

After several switchbacks your trail takes a fairly steady course south, still gradually climbing through extensive stands of burly whitebarks. Between the scattered trees you get full views of Shasta, including the Wintun and Hotlum Glaciers. The track crosses a few dry ravines and then comes to the fairly reliable flows of Brewer Creek. Snow will provide a bridge across this creek until at least early July, though take care that such a bridge is thick and strong enough.

From Brewer Creek the trail contours south 0.5 mile and then peters out. You might notice remnants of an old, illegally built jeep road that once continued up to 8,300 feet. At that elevation you can find decent camping spots and on up to about 9,000 feet. Beyond there, skiers and snowboarders can find summer snow to schuss on, typically into August.

TRIP 5 Ash Creek Falls Cross-Country Hike
DISTANCE AND DIFFICULTY: 2.5 miles round-trip, difficult

From the Brewer Creek Trail an experienced hiker can trek to Ash Creek Falls, Shasta's prettiest waterfall. This extension hike requires some cross-country route finding and scrambling.

From the area where the Brewer Creek Trail peters out atop a sandy ridge, contour south and then drop into a large, dry ravine. Climb back out of the ravine and contour around the next ridge at the 7,800-foot level. Curve west at that contour, and you'll soon pass beside a drop from where the falls are partly visible. The best views are from across the canyon, however. To reach there you'll have to angle down to cross the stream above the falls. Take extreme care to find the easiest way down this slope; if you are on-route, only a very short cliff near the bottom will require some scrambling. To cross the drainage again, take care; historically hikers have found deep snow forming a sturdy, convenient bridge over the creek, typically into late summer. Once across you can reach viewpoints by climbing directly upslope through a band of whitebarks.

TRIP 6 North Gate

DISTANCE AND DIFFICULTY: 6.5 miles round-trip, difficult

Into the 1980s this trail was just a boot track worn by climbers, but with extra traffic the U.S. Forest Service constructed a nice trail that's a great choice for a day hike, an overnight at the panoramic knolls and moraines below the glaciers, or access to the famed Hotlum Glacier.

The trail begins by climbing a gully southwest through an old clearcut, then continues into prime Shasta red fir forest. Before long the path turns west across a ravine in the shade of the stately trees and climbs out of this ravine onto the forested crest of the big lava flow that spilled down here a few thousand years ago. The track curves to the crest of the flow and turns back south to enter the realm of whitebark pines. Here grow some of the most magnificent whitebarks you'll find anywhere— stout, proud, and classically contorted mountain trees that show the golden wood of tissue that has succumbed to the high-altitude harshness. As you travel higher, on your right you will see a swath of these whitebarks laid flat by an avalanche that roared off the steep slope to the south in the heavy winter of 1997.

The sandy track continues climbing gradually through a defile between the avalanche slope and Point 8,852, which is a small, recently formed dacite dome. You soon leave the trees behind and gain the harsher ground of higher altitude as you curve south and climb a steady, steep grade into a broader and rockier valley. The view of Mount

Shasta's most symmetrical facet (and most recently formed cone) comes closer with every step. Soon you'll hear and then see a reliable stream tumbling through the rocks.

At about 9,500 feet you'll cross to the west side of the stream, and then you'll start to see bivouac and tent sites cleared on the little benches in this area. From this height, distant views to the northwest open up over the debris mounds of Shasta Valley to Preston Peak and the Siskiyous, and to the north well into southern Oregon, including Mount McLoughlin and the Klamath Falls territory.

If you continue climbing, the track will take you to midsummer snow line at about 10,000 feet. The Hotlum Glacier rises straight above, and the Bolam Glacier flows down the slopes to your right. Whether you camp or turn back for the trailhead, please take extra care to preserve the purity of the snowmelt stream here.

North Gate Trail

TRIP 7 Whitney Falls

DISTANCE AND DIFFICULTY: 3.4 miles round-trip, moderately difficult

Whitney Falls is a fascinating spot, where the outflow from the Whitney Glacier—often laden with debris—pours over a 250-foot-high cliff. This hike takes you to a good viewpoint within 0.3 mile of the falls. The hike gains about 1,000 feet, but washouts make for short sections of rough going. The volunteer Mount Shasta Trail Association works hard to maintain this trail. Overall, open scenery and solitude make this a pleasant excursion, though during midsummer this sunny trail can be baking hot. Note that this is not the way to get to the Whitney Glacier.

Begin by crossing Bolam Creek's dry wash just west of the trailhead, and then turn south to travel up the west side of this shallow drainage. Phlox, sulphur flower, and paintbrush dot this sandy track, and scattered Jeffrey pines, antelope brush, and mountain mahogany thinly cover the surrounding hills. Half a mile from the trailhead your path switchbacks up out of the drainage into full view of Shasta and the Bolam Glacier, and to the north you see across Shasta Valley to the northern Siskiyous.

Continue south along the west rim of Bolam Creek's dry ravine for a bit, then bend east to climb a couple of switchbacks. These take you south back across the drainage to a steady climb to another switchback. At this switchback the track heads west into a ravine shaded by a grove of Jeffrey pines and white firs.

From the shaded ravine the trail climbs steeply around a small ridge, then turns south a short distance to the brink of the impressively eroded canyon of Whitney Creek. The falls plunge off an overhanging cliff at the head of the canyon, and if you listen carefully, you'll hear rocks, gravel, and mud clattering over the cliff; Whitney Falls is anything but a clear stream, as glacial silt and Shasta's unstable, ashy debris readily dissolve into the flow. During recent hot summers the Whitney Glacier has released outburst floods (see the Geology chapter) that have poured over the falls and continued downstream to damage property beyond US 97. The loose canyon walls below you show ample evidence of undercutting by these floods. Return to your car via the same track.

TRIP 8 Circum-Shasta Backpack
DISTANCE AND DIFFICULTY: 25.0–35.0 miles, very difficult

Hiking around Mount Shasta is arguably the best way to get to know the mountain. In fact, John Muir wrote:

> far better than climbing [Mount Shasta] is going around its warm, fertile base, enjoying its bounties like a bee circling around a bank of flowers. . . . As you sweep around so grand a center, the mountain itself seems to turn. . . . One glacier after another comes into view, and the outlines of the mountain are ever changing.

Shasta's most notable circumnavigation was an expedition led by Dr. Clinton Hart Merriam in the summer of 1898. With other members of the U.S. Biological Survey, Merriam here finalized his pioneering (we would say "ecological" today) theory of life zones that correlate communities at higher elevations and higher latitudes. Merriam remains an iconic figure in American natural history. He also named Diller Canyon for Joseph Diller, a geologist who had recently studied Shasta.

Today still relatively few people take this ultimate Shasta backpack, partly because it's a fairly committing excursion through remote territory, with no trail to follow. In terms of route finding, strenuousness, and terrain, it should be considered a moderate and long mountaineering endeavor. Carrying an ice ax and knowing how to self-arrest can be important in the early season high around Shastina, and most hikers will make daily use of an altimeter and compass as they follow the map. Shasta's relatively open slopes help make route finding fairly easy for someone with experience, but soft, ashy footing occasionally gets tedious. One needs to plan the hike carefully to camp at water sources and to find passages across some of the canyons. Rewards include superb views essentially the whole way, crossing the toes of several glaciers, and especially coming to know the whole of this great mountain. Short side trips to view various waterfalls, in particular Whitney and Ash Creek Falls, are well worth the extra time. With these cautions in mind, confident backpackers who are comfortable with occasional scrambling should not be deterred from taking one of California's finest and least appreciated backcountry hikes. Fit hikers can complete the route in four days, and five would be comfortable for most backpackers.

Different hikers choose to circle the mountain at different elevations. A clockwise direction is preferred, usually beginning and ending at the Sierra Club Foundation cabin at Horse Camp. This way water sources, campsites, and scenery continually improve, and most of the tiresome scree is dealt with initially. There are many route variations, especially on the mountain's west flanks, but most hikers stay near the 8,000-foot level—approximately treeline. What follows is a general description of a recommended route, with mention of key canyon crossings and camp areas.

Starting from Horse Camp, you can stay low, perhaps planning a first camp at Cascade Gulch or Diller Canyon. In dry years these canyons might not offer water, though you can always count on finding snow to melt in Diller Canyon. The other good choice is to go high for a short first day and spend the first night in Hidden Valley (upper Cascade Gulch), where water is always available. This enables a higher traverse around Shastina, over spurs at 9,300 and then 9,100 feet. Staying high gives you a wonderfully scenic and somewhat shorter route, but it takes you across a couple of trying scree slopes, and you have to negotiate some short cliff bands, 0.25 mile south of Diller Canyon and about 0.75 mile north of it. In any case, be aware that it's a very long way around Shastina between good water sources—potentially all the way from Cascade Gulch to Bolam Creek.

To traverse the Graham Creek–Bolam Creek area, it's best to avoid the morainal hills below the Whitney and Bolam Glaciers by going somewhat high across the terminus of the Whitney Glacier. There are springs and small grassy areas for good camping west of the Whitney Glacier toe, but they can be difficult to find. For those who go high, a reliable camp awaits in the basin below the Bolam Glacier, at about 9,600 feet. From this camp it's best to descend along the east side of Bolam Creek to treeline.

In the North Gate vicinity, most hikers contour south of Point 8,852 and gradually lose elevation as they continue east. A higher option is to climb over the morainal benches near Point 9,535, where there's excellent camping on flat, sandy ground and almost always snowmelt. To continue east off these benches, descend a sandy gully through some cliff bands east-southeast of Point 9,535 and contour toward Gravel Creek. Those who are relatively high will find difficulty in crossing Gravel Creek's canyon. The canyon is a deep land-slash with walls of steep, unstable ash and precarious boulders. Members of a party going up and down these slopes must take special care to avoid knocking rocks onto one another, as well as not to climb directly below or above one another. Below 7,500 feet these canyon walls are safer and not as high.

The next key point is Ash Creek right above the falls. To get there, hike through whitebark parklands near the 8,000-foot level across Brewer Creek (which is reliable and clear). Contour around the ridge just north of the falls at 7,800 feet and then cut back west to descend into the canyon above the falls. An 8-foot cliff on this descent requires some scrambling. Solid snow—avalanche debris—usually offers a convenient bridge across Ash Creek until late in summer. On the south side of the canyon, climb directly upslope through a band of whitebarks.

Cold Creek, Pilgrim Creek, and Clear Creek are all reliable and silt-free. Contour around Clear Creek's canyon at about 7,800 feet to set up for the crucial crossing of intimidating Mud Creek canyon. From around 7,700 feet on the canyon rim, drop straight into the canyon on a loose, sandy rib at the uppermost grove of full-size firs, just upcanyon from a bare landslide area. Near the canyon bottom, again take special care to avoid sending rocks onto partners. Cross Mud Creek a couple of hundred yards above the falls, and climb directly up a steep, faint, side drainage to get back out of the canyon. This exit is important; large rocks offer reliable stepping-stones to the rim. From the southwest rim of the canyon, a course that contours near 7,800 feet will take you around Red Fir Ridge to South Gate Creek. The lush meadows are among the nicest campsites on the mountain. From here you can rise to The Gate on South Gate Meadows Trail. After this you can either stay high to meet the Everitt Memorial Highway at the Old Ski Bowl or contour southwest to meet the highway at Panther Meadows Campground. At the road, of course, you can choose how to complete your trip. You can conclude the hike here, or take an unmarked use trail along the north side of Everitt Memorial Highway down to Bunny Flat.

Green Butte Ridge *(photographed by Chris Carr/Shasta Mountain Guides)*

SHASTA'S GEOLOGY

Most of us recognize that Mount Shasta is a volcano, a "fire mountain" formed by seething hot rock erupting from the interior of the earth. Indeed, Shasta is among the larger of the many scores of volcanoes that ring the entire Pacific basin. The volcanoes in this region are the result of a process that begins when the Pacific seafloor spreads east and west. When the ever-expanding seafloor runs up against a continental landmass, it is forced into the earth's hot interior, where it melts. This molten magma works its way up to the surface; where it pushes up through the earth's crust, a volcano forms.

The earliest eruptions in the Shasta area helped form Everitt Hill, just south of Shasta, about 450,000 years ago. The eruptions that formed Mount Shasta itself started between 400,000 and 300,000 years ago. In geologic terms this makes Shasta quite young—younger than many of the other volcanoes in the Cascades. In fact, when Shasta was forming, the local environment must have closely resembled the one that we know today.

As the mountain grew to roughly its current height, it collected lots of snowfall and large glaciers. Then, about 350,000 years ago, the mountain collapsed, releasing one of the largest landslides in known geologic history. A significant percentage of the peak sloughed off and crashed northwest across Shasta Valley, past the current site of Yreka, and temporarily choked off the Klamath River. When you're up on the Hotlum or

Bolam Glaciers, or at another Shasta vantage looking northwest, you can see the legacy of this cataclysmic episode: a landscape of debris, randomly forming hills spanning some 170 square miles. Though an earthquake or small eruption might have triggered the avalanche, none of the current evidence suggests this is what happened. It may have simply been the fall of an oversteepened or weakened slope. On the mountain's opposite, southeast side, the deeply eroded Mud Creek Canyon and its Konwakiton headwall are the standing remnants of proto–Mount Shasta.

After this calamity, additional eruptions, through a sequence of three new vents, rebuilt the mountain as a collection of cones and formed the Mount Shasta we now know and love. (A vent is the opening on a volcano from which lava, gases, and other volcanic material escape; visualize a smoldering hole at the top or on the side of a mountain.) The first "new" vent started erupting around 250,000 years ago, forming the Sargents Ridge–Avalanche Gulch side of the mountain. This vent ceased long ago, and at least two periods of glaciation "swept out" the Avalanche Gulch and Ski Bowl basins; the steepened ridges we see today are the remains of that cone.

Next came the adjacent Misery Hill vent, which spewed up enough material to create the namesake bane of Avalanche Gulch climbers who crest the Red Banks and find, at 13,000 feet, that they have another substantial slope to climb. Approximately 9,500 years ago, in its final gasp, this vent spilled out the molten cinders that congealed into the Red Banks, the brow of pumice that caps Avalanche Gulch. Around the same time the next new vent opened to the west, forming Shastina. Toward the end of Shastina's formation, either a collapsing eruption or a violent out-blast excavated the gash we now call Diller Canyon, sending debris onto what's now the site of the city of Weed.

Shasta's most recent eruptions have come from the Hotlum vent, forming the current summit area and the mountain's northern flanks. One impressive feature created by this most recent vent is the Military Pass lava flow, which poured down Inconstance Creek several thousand years ago, reaching all the way down to an elevation of about 6,100 feet and forming lobes that are striking today even on a topo map. The Hotlum vent has continued erupting on average every 250–350 years, creating flows that have formed the steplike terraces where northside climbers often camp. (Note that a lava "flow" can refer to lava that is molten or solidified.) The (very) hot, acidic springs and sulfurous gas vents just northwest of Shasta's summit crags testify that this cone's plumbing is still active. However, accounts from 19th-century climbers described a much more extensive array of them.

Geologists are still uncovering clues as to when Shasta last erupted. For a long time it was thought that the mountain erupted in the late 1700s, and it was widely discussed whether the diaries of the famous French mariner Jean de La Pérouse described a glimpse of that eruption from his ship. New isotopic methods of dating volcanic rocks, however, date the most recent debris on Shasta to around 1,800 years ago.

We can say for sure, however, that over the last couple of millennia, Shasta has erupted more frequently than any other Cascade volcano. Collectively, Shasta's multiple cones form the largest mountain by volume in the whole Cascade chain—some 84–120 cubic miles of debris regurgitated from the earth's mantle and crust. This is interesting because the other largest mountains in the chain cluster farther north in Washington. Chemical analysis confirms that the lava that formed Shasta came from deep within the earth's mantle, collecting crust material on its way up.

Shasta's legacy tells us that it will erupt again, though no one can say when or how severely. U.S. Geological Survey constantly monitors seismic tremors and deformations that could signal a coming eruption, and as of this writing the most recent and notable swarm of quakes beneath Shasta was detected in the summer of 2013.

Shasta's Glaciers

Mountain glaciers form in snowy/cold climates where more snow accumulates during the winter than can melt during the summer. Over decades the accumulated snow piles up, compacts into ice, and gains enough mass to start creeping and flowing downhill. The river of ice rides down with almost irresistible force, accumulating loose rocks and grinding down bedrock along the way. Eventually, the glacier's front reaches a lower elevation where warmer air melts it away. Thus, a glacier could be considered a gravity-driven system that dissipates "excess" snowfall.

Glaciers wax and wane with changes in temperature and snowfall. A persistent cooling or warming of just a few degrees will bring on or end a glacial advance, as will an increase or decrease in accumulating snow. When Shasta formed 350,000 years ago, the northern hemisphere had cooler and snowier conditions than today, so glaciers must have periodically draped and scoured the mountain since its inception.

Geologists can estimate the previous size of a glacier in part by analyzing the distinguishing mounds of debris (moraines) that the ice rivers left behind. Moraines around Shasta reveal that, during at least one glacial period, ice from the mountain's south slopes merged in Strawberry Valley with ice from Mount Eddy. This combined glacier then may have flowed close to the present-day site of Dunsmuir. In the north, glaciers pooled in Shasta Valley.

The climate at Shasta has, at times, been warm and dry enough to completely melt the glaciers. At about the same time Shastina was forming, a warm and dry period began that melted all the permanent ice on the mountain. Geologists think there were at least a few glacial advances after that, between 9,000 and 3,000 years ago, but the really big glaciation ended by 6,000 years ago. For a couple of thousand years, then, Shasta probably held little or no ice. Starting about 4,000 years ago, a cooler and wetter period caused fairly extensive glaciers to re-form on the mountain, probably even on its sunnier south slopes. This "neo-glaciation" continued strong into the late 1700s and then started waning during the 19th century. At the turn of the 20th century Shasta's glaciers briefly resurged, but soon after that a few warm, dry decades dramatically diminished them. The Wintun Glacier especially dwindled to just a vestige of stagnant ice. It wasn't until the 1940s that heavier snowfalls returned and somewhat rejuvenated the glaciers. For instance, by 1972 the Whitney Glacier extended more than 1,500 feet beyond its much more withered position of 1944.

Today at least eight distinct glaciers flow down the sides of Mount Shasta, including the largest ones—by far—in California. The Whitney Glacier is the longest in the state and a true valley glacier, pouring down between Shasta and Shastina and carting away debris that falls from the flanks of both sides. As it undercuts Shastina's east flanks, the Whitney creates a lot of rockfall. It also spills over a couple of very steep sections, causing its ice to fracture into blocky, spectacular icefalls. The feast-or-famine–type snowfall in recent years probably accounts for the Whitney Glacier's advances during 2003–2005, and retreats since then.

Shasta's largest glacier by volume is the Hotlum, which flows northeast from near the summit. The Hotlum also cracks over two or three icefalls. Relatively dry years since the 1920s have isolated a lobe of the Hotlum, and this is often referred to as the Chicago Glacier because of the extensive studies conducted on it by University of Chicago researchers.

The Wintun Glacier on the east side has a fairly active core section that forms a small icefall as it drops into Ash Creek's upper canyon. The Bolam Glacier is extensive too, but its few crevasses and its gently sloping, receding terminus show that it is relatively inactive.

Shasta's three other glaciers flow out of small, sheltered cirques in the mountain's southeast headwalls. The Konwakiton and Mud Creek Glaciers (the latter also known as the Stuhl Glacier) spill out of small basins above Mud Creek; notably, the Konwakiton is especially active and fractured for its small size. The Watkins Glacier commemorates amateur geologist R. Harry Watkins Jr., a local resident who described the glacier and the general post-1940 rejuvenation of Shasta's glaciers long before "official" geologists took notice. Careful observers have noticed that during recent snowy periods, an area to the left side of Avalanche Gulch, above Lake Helen, and beneath Casaval Ridge shows signs of rocks being carried by ice underneath. This could qualify it as a rock glacier, and some have taken to calling it Olberman Glacier in honor of Mac Olberman, a mountaineer and Horse Camp custodian who identified the presence of ice up there in the 1920s.

The last few decades have seen wilder fluctuations between wet and dry years than in the past. Shasta's glaciers have responded, though not as simply as we might predict. Snowpack surges from heavy winters take a few years to make their way to lower elevations, warmer winters can actually bring more moisture and snowfall to the highest elevations, and warmer summers can induce faster motion, temporary lengthening, and thinning. No one has recently taken on the detailed, long-term measurements of snow accumulation, or the extent, thickness, and rates of ice movement on Shasta's glaciers. But photographic evidence over a scale of decades suggests that the volume and extent of ice on Shasta has diminished, as it has for most glaciers around the globe.

Hot summers occasionally cause Shasta's glaciers to release outburst floods, referred to by the Icelandic term *jökulhlaups*. These happen when high melting flows get dammed within a glacier and then burst free. Shasta's most infamous *jökulhlaups* happened in 1924, when a flow gushed out of the Konwakiton and Mud Creek Glaciers, collected mud and rocks from Mud Creek's unstable canyon walls, then spewed itself far enough beyond the mountain to damage structures in nearby McCloud. Mud, silt, rocks, and boulders from the floods spread many feet deep through the forests near McCloud, damaged buildings and buried railroad tracks in the town, muddied the McCloud River, continued far down the Sacramento River, and, according to a U.S. Forest Service report, even clouded San Francisco Bay. Observers estimated that the Konwakiton lost 0.375 mile during that summer. Smaller outburst floods have raced down most of Shasta's canyons in recent decades; some from the Whitney Glacier have even covered US 97 and threatened homes to the north, and others have again damaged McCloud.

Shasta's glaciers will change, rocks will fall, and, of course, the apparently quiet and stable mountain we know today will erupt again. So when you hike, climb, or ski on this great mountain, know that it is a dynamic being.

SHASTA'S FLORA AND FAUNA

Soaring high above the Northern California landscape, Mount Shasta stands as a de facto island to many special plants and animals. Living things here have to adapt to an unusual range of conditions, starting with a dramatically seasonal climate where summers are fairly dry and winters bury everything above 6,000 feet or so with 20–40 feet of snow. What makes Shasta even more challenging to live on is that most of the snow-melt percolates through the porous volcanic soils, leaving the slopes surprisingly dry, almost desertlike. This seasonality and aridity make it an especially tough place to survive; compared to neighboring volcanoes Lassen Peak and the Crater Lake highlands, notably fewer plant species grow on Shasta.

Any explorer will notice how the character of the vegetation on Shasta changes with elevation. Indeed, its peak is like a cone-shaped model of ecological transition. A summer's study on Mount Shasta in 1898 was enough for naturalist Clinton Hart Merriam to theorize that a higher altitude has an equivalent environment, flora, and fauna to a higher latitude. The concept is, of course, a simplification, but a thousand feet of altitude roughly corresponds to 100 miles of latitude. On Shasta, in one sweep we can identify five of the West's six life zones: Upper Sonoran (chaparral and oaks), Transition (pinewoods), Canadian (fir forests), Hudsonian (hemlock and whitebark groves), and finally, as we look up to the higher reaches, Arctic-Alpine (alpine meadows and rock and ice).

In Shasta's lower slopes, up to 5,500 feet or so, plants gather moisture from cool, rainy winters to burst out and then endure hot, dry summers. Most of these lower slopes are covered with chaparral, especially green-leaf manzanita and tobacco brush, a ceanothus. Other shrubs include oaklike chinquapin, buckbrush ceanothus, antelope brush, and western chokecherry. From a distance the chaparral appears as a pleasant green rug reaching up the mountain. Among the bushes grow flowers including penstemons, gilias, and the queen of Shasta's flowers, the Shasta lily. The year of his study, Merriam observed that "Shasta rises from a forested region, and the mountain itself is continuously forest-covered up to an altitude of 7,500 feet or 8,000 feet." The aggressive, sun-loving brush has taken over since loggers cleared the ponderosa pines and white firs, but since the Great Depression the U.S. Forest Service has been planting orderly rows of ponderosa pines, hoping with marginal success to speed the return of marketable timber.

Above 5,500 feet, cooler temperatures and heavier precipitation allow conifers to gradually become dominant. Towering over the shrubs are the long-needled branches of ponderosa pine, the "Christmas tree" spires of white fir and Douglas-fir, the splayed branches of sugar pine, and the cone rosettes of knobcone pine. This forest grows most richly on Shasta's southern slopes, whereas sparser trees and brush dominate the drier northwest side. On the northeast side, a slower-growing forest of lodgepole pines struggles against the inland influence of colder, drier winters.

In the heavy snowbelt between 6,000 and 8,000 feet, one majestic tree dominates—Shasta red fir. Closely related to the red fir of the Sierra and the noble fir of the Northwest, the Shasta red fir grows curved combs of blue-green needles and furrowed maroon bark over a solid, unbranched trunk. Shasta red fir is distinguished by cones with papery bracts hanging

Shasta red fir cones

from each seed envelope, and its needles and bark differ subtly. In the dry duff underneath the firs, scattered herbs such as white-veined wild ginger, mountain violet, and the delicate pink steer's head grow. In the mountains farther south, you won't find Shasta red fir until you reach the southern Sierra. This disjointed distribution probably dates from the Pleistocene, when glaciers and a snowy climate likely eliminated the Shasta red fir from most of the Sierra. In more recent decades, of course, logging has hauled out a lot of Shasta red fir wood.

Practically synonymous with the snowy Cascades is the delicate nodding tip of the mountain hemlock; thank the moist pockets on Shasta for fostering this graceful tree. In upper South Gate Valley, diminutive hemlocks dominate. Just above, on the east slopes of Gray Butte, some tall, stout hemlocks compare in stature with red firs. Isolated mountain hemlocks sprout up around treeline, about 8,500 feet.

The aridity of Shasta's soils is most obvious in the openings in the montane forest. At snowy elevations elsewhere in California and Oregon, you see green carpets, but on Shasta the meadows are sandy. Generally two plants grow well here: silver lupine, with its purple flower-spikes, and Bloomer's rabbitbush, with its scraggly yellow petals. The minty fragrance of pennyroyal usually wafts through these clearings, and even a casual scan finds paintbrush, phlox, mountain buckwheat, arnica, or pussypaws adding summer color between the little shrubs. A few rare plants live in some of these clearings too. Mount Shasta arnica grows only in the Shasta and Crater Lake areas, and Shasta knotweed grows only here and to the south, in the northern Sierra. *Phacelia cookei*, a member of the waterleaf family named after Shasta's premier botanist, Dr. William Bridge Cook, grows only on the lower north slopes of Mount Shasta. These endemic species probably evolved in recent millennia as Shasta's island habitat grew.

Lush meadows thrive along the profuse springs of Panther and South Gate Creeks. Sogginess here keeps the trees at bay, while rushes, sedges, and mountain heather flourish. One rare plant, Shasta bluebell (also known as Wilkins' harebell), grows only at the springs at the head of Panther Creek, at the springs on Spring Hill behind Horse Camp, and in the Trinity Alps.

Above about 8,000 feet you come to the magical highland where austere trees tough out severe winters, late-lying snow, and intense summer radiation. The high tree on Shasta is the whitebark pine. Whitebarks endure and even thrive in extensive parklands here, and on Shasta's north and east slopes many reach 30–60 feet tall; some scattered specimens rival the largest whitebarks ever measured. Higher than around 8,500 feet, the whitebarks huddle together in thickets barely 3 feet high. These ground forests reach their highest elevations along Shasta's exposed ridgecrests, up to 9,500 feet, where winter snows melt early and allow a longer growing season. The risk of such exposed perches is that the needles need snow for protection from winter's blasting winds, and after drought winters, many of these "hedges" show extensive die-back.

Perennial wildflowers grow among the whitebarks and at even higher elevations. Gray's campion, alpine buckwheat, Shasta knotweed, spreading phlox, Lyall's lupine, and others splash color across high, sandy slopes. In the brief summer growing season, these hardy plants somehow suck moisture from stony earth that, for most other plants, has long since dried up. Probably the most common alpine flower is the showy white windflower, which nods over ash and talus fields alike. Talus also shelters "softer" plants like mountain heather, alpine sorrel, and timberline phacelia. The toughest of Shasta's high flowers is Jacob's ladder, a tender-looking herb whose snow-white blossoms grow in rock crevices over 13,000 feet. Its

Whitebark pine broken by winds

wormlike leaves are thick, spongy, and finely hairy to store nutrients and retain water.

Life stretches to almost miraculous heights on Shasta. Colorful lichens crust over rocks nearly to the summit, and in summer you might notice snow with a pink tint—that's *Chlamydomonas nivalis*, snow algae. Incredibly, another alga has been identified in the mud of Shasta's summit hot springs. Withstanding temperatures up to 135°F and an acidity as strong as battery acid (pH 1), *Cyanidium caldarium* somehow sustains itself in the fumaroles on moisture, minerals, and sunlight.

Shasta knotweed *(photographed by Scott Loarie/Flickr/CC BY 2.0 [creativecommons .org/licenses/by/2.0])*

The Fauna

Birds

Birdwatchers may spy up to 200 species of birds on Mount Shasta, some living year-round on the mountain, some spending spring and summer here to nest, and some just passing through. During spring and summer a cacophony of songbirds feed on the abundant seeds, insects, and nectar. Sparrows, warblers, towhees, bluebirds, solitaires, and more alight on branches and proclaim their territory, breeding and rearing their young on Shasta's lower slopes.

In the forests songbirds are less numerous but still common, calling down quiet corridors between the big trees. Most any day you'll hear the ringing twitters and winsome mating whistles of the mountain chickadee. This bandit-faced bird gleans insects from red fir boughs. Other calls echoing through the firs include the nasal "tin horn" notes of red-breasted nuthatches; the long, warbled songs of flycatchers; and the screeches and cries of two bold cousins, the Steller's jay and the gray jay. Woodpeckers drum on the firs, both to announce their territory and drill for insects; most are hairy and white-headed woodpeckers. Nightfall often brings the haunting calls of great horned owls.

Up among the whitebarks, Clark's nutcrackers dominate, both in numbers and with their brash, jay-family squawking. The nutcrackers gather whitebark pine nuts, eating some off the trees and storing many for later, thereby planting the next generation. If you wear red, you'll likely attract hummingbirds, which hope you're a gigantic penstemon. Both Anna's and rufous hummingbirds make summer stopovers to feed on Shasta nectar before returning to tropical climes a few thousand miles south.

Raptors occasionally soar over Shasta and scan the slopes for rodents and reptiles. A binocular fix will most likely reveal red-tailed hawks, though golden eagles range here too, especially over the eastern slopes. A smaller, fast-flying raptor will probably be either a Cooper's hawk or a sharp-shinned hawk.

The lively little birds up high are finches. Cassin's finches twitter around treeline and above, snagging bugs off whitebarks. Gray-crowned rosy-finches roam to any elevation they please, scooping insects from the glaciers and often chirping to climbers. Mount Shasta is one of California's few nesting sites for the gray-cheeked (or Hepburn's) rosy-finch.

Mammals

Explorers don't often see mammals on Shasta, but tracks, scats, burrows, and middens indicate that they are around. Most common are chipmunks and squirrels. Chipmunks are dainty, with black and white "racing" stripes running down their backs and across their eyes. Most chipmunks on Shasta are yellow-pine chipmunks. They share the chaparral and forests up to about 7,000 feet with a similarly striped but chubbier golden-mantled ground squirrel. This animal stores up fat for a long hibernation, but the slender chipmunk stores a cache of food to fuel waking activities during winter's warm spells.

Romping through the trees is the lively Douglas squirrel. The red fir groves are alive with its long, shrilling calls and its comical *phews*. Shasta is also home to northern flying squirrels, though very few people witness this animal's nighttime glides. During a hike you might flush out one of two large rabbit species on Shasta. If the ears are particularly long, it's a black-tailed hare; if the ears seem average, but the body seems really big and you're at treeline or higher, it's probably a snowshoe hare. In Hidden Valley there are pikas: small, rabbitlike creatures that live only at cool elevations.

The best-known large mammal on Shasta is the black-tailed deer. It migrates with the seasons, following new growth up the mountain and nibbling especially on ceanothus leaves and new fir needles.

Sierra Nevada red fox *(photographed by U.S. Forest Service Region 5/Flickr/CC BY 2.0 [creativecommons.org/licenses/by/2.0])*

Coyotes range all over Shasta, even up to the whitebarks. The gray fox tends to stay in the midelevation forests and the chaparral, mixing a diet of rodents with manzanita berries. The Sierra Nevada red fox is a larger animal and is protected by the State of California due to its threatened status. In years past red foxes were seen around South Gate and Panther Meadow, but we haven't seen much of them recently.

A burrow on Shasta anywhere below 7,500 feet and about 8 inches in diameter will likely indicate the home of a badger. Badgers are low-slung, powerful animals that root out rodents from underground. The marten, a weasel relative of the badger, is a tan-colored tree climber the size of a small dog that hunts with amazing guile and quickness. Mountain lions roam Shasta, and the authors have seen tracks on Shasta's north flanks. Lions prey chiefly on deer, and they no doubt move up and down the mountain with their targets. Black bears also live in the chaparral and forest zones on Shasta. They eat just about anything, but thankfully we know of no instance on Shasta of bears getting into hikers' supplies.

AMENITIES, CONTACTS, AND OTHER INFORMATION

General Visitor Information

The towns at the foot of Mount Shasta have a full range of supplies, services, food, and lodging. You can obtain brochures and other useful information by visiting or calling the chamber of commerce or visitor center in each town:

Mt. Shasta
300 Pine St.
Mt. Shasta, CA 96067
530-926-4865
visitmtshasta.com

McCloud
303 Main St.
McCloud, CA 96057
530-964-3113
mccloudchamber.com

Dunsmuir
5915 Dunsmuir Ave.
Dunsmuir, CA 96025
530-235-2177
dunsmuir.com

Weed
34 Main St.
Weed, CA 96094
530-938-4624
weedchamber.com

For year-round weather, avalanche, and climbing information, an excellent source is shastaavalanche.org.

Mount Shasta is located within the Shasta–Trinity National Forest. The forest supervisor's office is at 3644 Avtech Pkwy., Redding, CA

96002; 530-226-2500. Two ranger district offices are in charge of the Shasta area, one in Mt. Shasta and one in McCloud. Wilderness, climbing, and campfire permits; trail guides; campground information; and various informative brochures are available at these offices. The Mt. Shasta Ranger Station maintains a complete visitor information facility. It also has a retail outlet for a wide selection of books, maps, guides, and even videos.

Mt. Shasta Ranger Station

204 W. Alma St.
Mt. Shasta, CA 96067
530-926-4511

Recorded recreational information line: 530-926-9613

Office hours: November–April, Monday–Friday, 8 a.m.–4:30 p.m.; May–October, Monday–Saturday, 8 a.m.–4:30 p.m.

McCloud Ranger Station

2019 Forest Road
McCloud, CA 96057
530-964-2184

Office hours: Monday–Friday, 8 a.m.–4:30 p.m.

The Mt. Shasta Ranger Station maintains the following campgrounds, which are open seasonally:

Castle Lake 10 miles southwest of Mt. Shasta on Castle Lake Road.

Gumboot 16 miles southwest of Mt. Shasta on South Fork Road (Forest Service Road 40N26).

McBride Springs 4.5 miles northeast of Mt. Shasta on Everitt Memorial Highway.

Panther Meadows 13.5 miles northeast of Mt. Shasta on Everitt Memorial Highway.

The McCloud Ranger Station maintains the following campgrounds, also open seasonally:

Ah-Di-Na 4 miles south of Lake McCloud, 16 miles south of CA 89.

Algoma 14 miles east of McCloud off CA 89.

Cattle Camp 11 miles east of McCloud off CA 89.

Fowlers Camp 6.5 miles east of McCloud off CA 89.

Harris Spring 17 miles north of Bartle off Harris Spring Road (County Road 15), off CA 89.

Trout Creek 20 miles northeast of McCloud on Pilgrim Creek Road/County Road 13, off CA 89.

Other campgrounds include:

Castle Crags State Park 20022 Castle Creek Road, Castella, CA 96017 (530-235-2684; parks.ca.gov/?page_id=454) There are 82 campsites, open year-round. The Pacific Crest Trail and many hiking trails run through the park.

Two privately owned campgrounds offer excellent facilities. Lake Siskiyou Resort & Camp, located 3 miles west of Mt. Shasta, has more than 300 campsites, including 150 RV sites, and you'll also find showers, a store, a marina, and a beach. There's excellent swimming in the lake, as well as boating, fishing, and windsurfing.

Lake Siskiyou Resort & Camp 4239 W. A. Barr Road, Mt. Shasta, CA 96067 (530-926-2610; reynoldsresorts.com /LakeSiskiyou.html)

A spacious KOA campground, conveniently located at the north end of the city of Mt. Shasta, has 110 campsites and complete facilities.

KOA Campground 900 N. Mt. Shasta Blvd., Mt. Shasta, CA 96067 (530-926-4029; koa.com/campgrounds/mount-shasta)

Driving Tours

The ranger district offices have many free maps and information on driving tours to points of interest in the area.

Museums

The Mt. Shasta Sisson Museum, located on the grounds of the Mt. Shasta Fish Hatchery, is open April–mid-December. Operated entirely by volunteers, the museum has many permanent displays on the history of Siskiyou County—particularly on Mount Shasta, both the city and the mountain—as well as temporary shows that change several times a year. The hatchery itself is the oldest operating one in California. You will enjoy seeing the giant, docile rainbow and brown trout swimming in its pools.

Mt. Shasta Sisson Museum 1 N. Old Stage Road, Mt. Shasta, CA 96067 (530-926-5508; mtshastamuseum.com) See website for seasonal hours.

The College of the Siskiyous Library in Weed has one of the most extensive special collections of books, manuscripts, photographs, and rare materials all pertaining to Mount Shasta, both the city and the mountain.

College of the Siskiyous 800 College Ave., Weed, CA 96094 (530-938-5331; siskiyous.edu/library/Shasta) Hours are by appointment for the Mount Shasta Collection.

Recreation

The following shops in Mt. Shasta carry and rent outdoor equipment, including ice axes, crampons, and boots for climbing. Reserve in advance for holiday weekends.

The Fifth Season 300 N. Mt. Shasta Blvd., Mt. Shasta, CA 96067 (530-926-3606; thefifthseason.com) The Fifth Season also has a 24-hour recorded phone message for the latest climbing and skiing conditions on the mountain: 530-926-5555.

Shasta Base Camp 308 S. Mt. Shasta Blvd., Mt. Shasta, CA 96067 (530-926-2359; shastabasecamp.com) Shasta Base Camp also has an indoor bouldering rock gym.

Guide Service

Shasta Mountain Guides (530-926-3117; shastaguides.com)

Downhill Skiing

Mt. Shasta Ski Park 4500 Ski Park Hwy., McCloud, CA 96057 (530-926-8610; snow phone: 530-926-8686; skipark.com) The park is 10 miles from I-5 via CA 89.

Cross-Country Skiing

Mt. Shasta Nordic Ski Organization Forest Service Road 31, Mt. Shasta, CA 96067 (530-925-3495; snow phone: 530-925-3494; mtshastanordic.org) It's 1 mile below Mt. Shasta Ski Park just off Ski Park Highway.

Snow Play Area

The U.S. Forest Service maintains a snow play area for sledding and sliding at Snowman's Hill, 6 miles east of I-5 on CA 89.

Other References

Hike Mt. Shasta (hikemtshasta.com) Trail information, directions, maps, and photos for hikers of all abilities.

Mt. Shasta Area Rock Climbing: A Climber's Guide to Siskiyou County by Grover Shipman (2013)

Mount Shasta Wildflowers (mountshastawildflowers.com) A field guide and plant list to Mount Shasta's wildflowers.

Mount Shasta Trail Association (mountshastatrailassociation .org) The Mount Shasta Trail Association is a nonprofit public benefit organization whose purpose is to design, construct, maintain, and use trails in the Mount Shasta area. The public is invited to participate in various trail projects, as well as scheduled hiking, canoeing, birding, and bicycling trips.

The Sierra Club Foundation Shasta Alpine Lodge (sierra clubfoundation.org; search "Horse Camp") The foundation's cabin at Horse Camp on Mount Shasta is one of the most popular base camps and hiking destinations, and the organization has an informative website and links.

Pacific Crest Trail Association (pcta.org) The PCTA maintains, preserves, and promotes the Pacific Crest Trail, including portions of the trail in the Mount Shasta region.

California Wilderness Coalition (calwild.org) The CWC is a nonprofit organization dedicated to preserving and enhancing California wilderness.

Siskiyou Land Trust (530-926-2259; siskiyoulandtrust .org) Promoting long-term land stewardship, preservation, and community projects in Siskiyou County.

Other Useful Information
Emergency Fire, police, ambulance, and highway patrol: Dial 911.

Road and Weather
Cal Trans, 24-hour report on road conditions: 800-427-7623

The latest weather information for the Shasta area is available from the following sources:

- The Fifth Season outdoor shop 24-hour climbing report: 530-926-5555

Mount Shasta Weather Websites:

- wunderground.com (enter "Mount Shasta, CA")

- weather.com (enter "Mount Shasta, CA")

- mountain-forecast.com (enter "Mount Shasta")

- shastaavalanche.org (many useful links)

- avalanche.org (click on "Mt. Shasta")

AFTERWORD

We're all guests, caretakers, and cohabitants of this planet. In the 21st century, environmental concern—and environmental degradation—has reached global proportions. Mount Shasta, like many other unique microenvironments, shows man's impact.

These commonsense guidelines apply to Mount Shasta, as well as other wilderness areas:

- Be a thoughtful backcountry visitor. Know something about your route and the area, and follow the management guidelines of the region's governing agencies.

- Accept the responsibility of knowing the basics of first aid, navigation, and minimum-impact camping.

- Choose your campsites thoughtfully, and leave them in as natural a state as possible. Keep groups small and blend camps and tents into the environment.

- Even where a fire is possible (and allowed), consider a fireless evening. Wildlands are feeling the effects of too many fires.

- Always use established latrines if they're available. If not, always use human waste pack-out bags.

- Do everything you can to protect water sources from contamination. Though giardia has not yet been reported on Mount Shasta, occurrences of it are increasing in the backcountry generally.

INDEX

access, hiker and climber. *See* hiker and climber access
acute mountain sickness (AMS), 18
American Indians and Mount Shasta, 6–7
animals and plants of Mount Shasta, 109–115
Ash Creek, 80, 101
Ash Creek Falls cross-country hike, 95–96
Avalanche Gulch, 41, 92, 104, 107
Avalanche Gulch climbing route, 30–38
avalanche hazards, 13, 67, 81

bathroom, 84, 122
bears, 115
bergschrunds, 33
birds, 113–114
Black Butte, 86
Bolam Glacier, 48, 51, 71, 97, 104, 107
Brewer Creek, 58
Brewer Creek Trail, 87, 95
Brewer, William, 50, 51
Brush, George Jarvis, 50
Bunny Flat, 40, 74, 76–77, 90, 101
Bunny Flat trailhead, 86

campgrounds, 117–118
camping on Mount Shasta, 17
Casaval Ridge climbing route, 41
Cascade Gulch climbing route, 42–43, 71
Castle Crags State Park, 118
Castle Lake, 80
cell phone service, 21
Chicago Glacier, 56, 107
chipmunks, 114
Circum-Shasta backpack trail, 99–101
Clarence King Lake, 34, 42, 43
Clear Creek, 63, 81, 87, 101
Clear Creek climbing route, 61–62
Clear Creek Trail, 87, 93–95
climber access. *See* hiker and climber access
climbing difficulty ratings, 28–29
climbing Mount Shasta
    camping, 17
    descending, 15–16
    introduction, physical fitness and training, 9–10
    ropes, rockfalls, rescues, 20–21
    route finding, 14–15
    teammates, team awareness, 11
    terrain skills, conditions awareness, 11–13
    trip-planning skills, 16
    weather awareness, 14
climbing regulations, 84–85
climbing routes. *See also specific route*
    climbing difficulty ratings, 28–29
    descending eastside routes, 57–61
    east and southeast sides, 61–63
    generally, 27–28
    north and northeast sides, 53–57
    Shastina to Hotlum-Bolam Ridge, 44–52
    skiing, 69–74
    southwest side from Sargents Ridge to Cascade Gulch, 30–43
College of the Siskiyous Library, Weed, 119
Colonna, Benjamin, 47
commercial ski areas and lift-serviced, 79–80
compasses, 15
Cooke, Dr. William Bridge, 111
Cousins, Alice, 47
coyotes, 115
crampons, 12, 13
cross-country skiing, 120

descending Mount Shasta, 15–16
difficulty ratings, climbing, 28–29
Diller Canyon, 44, 78, 99, 100, 104
Diller, Joseph, 78, 99
Douglas squirrel, 114
downhill skiing, 119
driving tours, 118

eastside routes, descending, 57–58
Eddy, Harriette Catherine, 30
Eddys, the, 80
emergencies, 21, 121
Everitt Memorial Highway, 38–39, 79, 87, 101
Everitt Memorial Highway, winter access, 74–78
Everitt, Samuel, 87

fauna (animals) of Mount Shasta, 109–113
Fay, Jerome, 35, 46
Fifth Season outdoor shop, 24, 80, 119
fires, 122
fitness for climbing, 9–10
flora (plants) of Mount Shasta, 109–113

geology of Mount Shasta, 103–108
giardia, 122
glaciers. *See also specific glacier*
    exploration and naming of Mount Shasta's, 50–51
    of Mount Shasta, 105–108

GPS devices, 15
Graham Creek-Bolam Creek area, 100
Gray Butte Northwest Face, 76
Green Butte, 91–92
Green Butte Ridge climbing route, 40, 70
guide service, 119

Heart rock field, the, 32
Helen Lake, 31, 32, 34, 38, 41
Hidden Valley, 42–43, 91, 100
high altitude issues on Mount Shasta,
    17–18, 20
hiker and climber access, 83
    trail descriptions, 88–101
    trailheads, 85–88
    wilderness permits, regulations, 83–84
Horse Camp, 19, 41, 42, 77, 80, 90–91, 100
Horse Camp Trail, 86, 88, 90–91
Hotlum Glacier, 8, 51, 52, 53–55, 72, 96,
    97, 103–104, 106–107
Hotlum Glacier climbing route, 53–56
Hotlum-Bolam Ridge
    from Shastina, 44–52
    climbing route, 72
Hotlum-Wintun Ridge climbing route,
    56–57, 72

John Muir climbing route, 30–38, 69–70
jökulhlaups, 107–108

Karuk tribe, 6, 7
King, Clarence, 42, 50–51
Klamath tribe, 5
Konwakiton Glacier, 32, 33, 36, 51, 61,
    94, 107, 108
    from the east climbing route, 62–63
    from the south climbing route, 63

Lake Helen, 107
Lake Siskiyou Resort & Camp, 118
LaLande, Jeff, 5
latrines, 122
Level (route descriptions), 69
lift-serviced and commercial ski areas, 79–80

mammals, 114–115
McCloud, 108, 116
Merriam, Dr. Clinton Hart, 99, 109, 110
Military Pass lava flow, 104
Misery Hill, 34, 36, 104
mountaineering teammates, team aware-
    ness, 11
mountain lions, 115

Mount Eddy, 30, 80, 106
Mount Hood, 5
Mount McLoughlin, 5, 6
Mount Shasta
    and American Indians, 6–7
    animals of, 109–113
    climbing. See climbing Mount Shasta
    climbing routes. See climbing routes
    contact information, 116, 117'
    descending eastside routes, 57–58
    described, 3–6
    exploration and naming of glaciers, 50–51
    first ascent, 30
    geology. glaciers of, 103–108
    illustrated, 11
    plants of, 109–113
    ski circumnavigation, 80–81
    skiing, snowboarding, & ski touring,
        65–81
    sulfur springs, 6–7
    Summit Monument, 46–47
    trailheads, 85–88
Mount Shasta Snowmen ski club, 79
Mt. Shasta Nordic Ski Organization, 120
Mt. Shasta Sisson Museum, 47, 118–119
Mt. Shasta Ski Bowl, 38, 39, 79–80, 87, 119
Mt. Shasta Wilderness, 83–84, 94
Mud Creek, 101
Mud Creek Canyon, 62, 81, 94, 104
Mud Creek Glacier, 40, 94, 107
Muir, John, 30, 35, 36, 46, 99
museums, 118–119

North Gate Trail, 88, 96

Ogden, Peter Skene, 5–6
Olberman, Mac, 31, 107
Olberman Glacier, 107
Old Ski Bowl, 75, 86, 101
Old Ski Bowl climbing route, 38–39, 70
outburst floods, 107–108

Panther Meadow, 75
Panther Meadow Campground, 101
Pearce, Elias D., 30
Pérouse, Jean de La, 4, 105
plants and animals of Mount Shasta, 109–115
Powder Bowl and Sun Bowl, 76
Powell, Major John Wesley, 51

ranger district offices, 117
ratings, climbing difficulty, 28–29
recreation, 119

Red Banks, 32, 34, 36, 37, 42, 69, 104
Red Fir Flat, 78
red foxes, 115
references, other, 120–121
rescues, 20–21
Rhodes, Phil, 3
road conditions, 85, 121
rockfalls, 20
Rogue River, 5
ropes for climbing, 20

Sacramento River, 4
Sand Flat alternative trailhead, 86
Sand Flat Area, 77–78
Sargent, John, 39
Sargents Ridge climbing route, 38, 39–40
Season (route descriptions), 69
self-arrest technique, 12
Shasta Base Camp, 119
Shasta bluebell, 111
Shasta red fir, 110–111
Shasta River, 5
Shasta-Shastina saddle, 45, 51, 66
Shasta tribe, 6, 7
Shasta-Trinity National Forest, 84
Shastina, 3, 4, 11, 43, 78, 106
   to Hotlum-Bolam Ridge, 44–52
   -Shasta saddle, 45, 51, 66
Sierra Club Foundation cabin, 31, 41, 42,
   77, 80
Simpson, George, 5
Siskiyou County Sheriff's Department, 28
Sisson Lake, 34
ski-in base camps for wilderness skiing, 79
skiing
   categories of, 67–68
   climbing routes, 69–74
   cross-country, 120
   downhill, 119
   generally, 65–69
ski touring generally, 65–69
Smith, Jedediah, 5
snow algae (Chlamydomonas nivalis), 113
snowboarding
   categories of, 67–68
   climbing routes, 69–74
   generally, 65–69
Snowman's Hill, 65, 66, 79
snow play area, 120
Southern Pacific Railroad, 79
South Gate Creek, 101
South Gate Meadows, 75

South Gate Meadows Trail, 86, 93
squirrels, 114
Steiner, Otto, 66
Stuhl, Edward, 1, 36
Stuhl Glacier, 107
sulfur fumaroles, 34
Summit Monument, 46–47
Summit Passes, 84
Sun Bowl and Powder Bowl, 76

Thumb Rock, 32, 39, 94
toilets, 84, 122
trail descriptions. See also specific trail
   hiker and climber access, 88–101
trailheads of Mount Shasta, 85–88
training for climbing, 9–10
trip-planning skills, 16

U.S. Biological Survey, 99

visitor information, 116–118

Wagon Camp, 76
Watkins Glacier, 61, 107
Watkins Jr., R. Harry, 107
weather
   awareness before climbing, 14
   Mount Shasta's, 23–24
   reports, road conditions, 121
Weed, 116
West Face climbing route, 42, 70
Whitney, Professor Josiah D., 44, 50, 51
Whitney Falls, 83, 98
Whitney Falls trailhead, 88
Whitney Glacier, 33, 34, 43, 71, 98, 100,
   106, 108
wilderness
   guidelines, 122
   permits, 28, 83–84
   regulations, 83–84
   skiing, ski-in base camps, 79
Wilkin's harebell, 111
winter access, Everitt Memorial Highway,
   74–78
Wintun Glacier, 51, 56–57, 60, 72, 106,
   107
Wintun Glacier climbing route, 58–60
Wintun Ridge climbing route, 60–61
Wintun tribe, 6, 7, 51, 58

ABOUT THE AUTHORS

Andy Selters is a mountaineer, writer, guide, and photographer with experience around the world. His other books include hiking guides to the Pacific Crest Trail and many parts of California's Sierra, the manual *Glacier Travel & Crevasse Rescue,* and the award-winning *Ways to the Sky: A Historical Guide to North American Mountaineering.* Currently he lives in Bishop, California, where he gets into the mountains when he can and catches a lot of fastballs from his teenage son.

California native **Michael Zanger** has been hooked on the mountains since a family trip to Yosemite at the age of 5. He founded Shasta Mountain Guides in the mid-1970s and has lived at the foot of Mount Shasta for nearly 50 years. In addition to his excursions on Mount Shasta, he has participated in climbs and expeditions in North and South America, Europe, Africa, and Asia. He is also the author of a book on the history of the mountain, *Mt. Shasta: History, Legend & Lore.*